SHARE MORE OF YOUR FAMILY'S STORY

SHARE MORE OF YOUR FAMILY'S STORY

TRACI GORMLEY

Edited by
MOLLY HOLT

PINK
CITRUS
BOOKS

Formatted and Published by Pink Citrus Books

Cover Design by Blue Water Books

Edited by Molly Holt, Edits by Molly

Proofread by Carri Flores

Contact Traci via Facebook

To My Children & Grandchildren

STARTING SMALL WITH A STORY

*T*his book will help you create and reframe your personal and family history into a *daily* strengthening story.

If you love genealogy, this book is for you. If you love your parents, siblings, cousins, children, grandchildren, and grandparents, this book is for you.

Do you want more good family memories or stories? Do you want to learn from your family? Do you want to help your family members feel better or give them new courage? Your family story, your personal story, has the power to lift and enlighten all of your family—if you will become a true storyteller. Let us learn how to tell our personal and family stories. Doing so creates enduring bonds that hold all of our family members together and strengthen us for more successes.

I want you to create and present stories that are easy and fun to read, offer encouragement, and empower your family. In this book, I offer suggestions that you can use to build family unity and strength. This book will guide you and cheer you on as you foster appreciation and love among your relatives. You will learn to use your time to tell your stories in a way that may just last for generations.

I am enthusiastic about genealogy and family history due, in part, to great storytelling. I'll read anything and everything on the subject. I reread the same family history magazine several times just to enjoy all over again the articles and pictures. I check Ancestry.com and Family Search like others check Facebook or Twitter. It is an irresistible urge to know more about my family and find another relative, document, story, or photo about my ancestors. I love to share pictures online and then see if anyone finds them and saves them to their own family tree.

And this love for genealogy isn't a new thing in my life; I have loved family history for as long as I can remember. I would listen intently as my grandmothers told me stories about their lives or my parents' lives. After our visits, I loved going home and replaying the stories in my mind at bedtime. I'd ask questions of my parents to see if I got the story right or if I missed something. I'd try and make them add to the story. It was never enough. I always wanted more family. Funny really, when you know I am the second child of eleven children.

My grandparents had pictures I wanted but couldn't take home. I remember the first time I picked up a photo of my great grandmother. It seemed like I was looking into a paper mirror. I instantly wanted to know this woman who I mirrored in every physical way. There was a connection.

Years later, I have boxes of folders with family photos, documents, and paper logs. On my computer, I have digital records of documents and photos. I have online accounts with —you guessed it—my ancestors' names, documents, and photos. I've inherited and created years of pedigree charts and family group sheets that date back to the 1980s. I transferred the information into software programs and transferred them again onto online genealogy sites.

It's not that I'm done finding and gathering my family history. I haven't finished my genealogy back to Adam and Eve with photos. But I want to come out of research and recording. I want to live and share the family stories. I want the history to help with the future.

I think about it like this: I want a big family dinner with everyone there, regardless of time. If you gathered around a dinner table with your first five generations, could you imagine the conversations, laughter, and topics? That's the dinner party I want to attend. I decided I needed to create that opportunity for my family. While I cannot create a physical gathering place for the people, there can be a place for their stories.

So how do we create a place for our family stories? I want it to be easy, natural, and inexpensive. It's a beginning.

Recently I borrowed my brother-in-law's family history book that his father had written twenty years ago. It is a hard bound book of 740 pages. It is an excellent family history, and I loved every minute reading it even though it wasn't my family. It is a history of his family from the 1770s to the early 1900s. It is brilliantly written and interwoven with American and religious history. It even has a forty-page index. It is every family historian's dream. I do wonder how much of the family has read it and if they loved it like I did. So many family members appreciate that it is done and that they have a finished product, but it doesn't make their heart sing.

It may be our goal or dream to write such a beautiful comprehensive history, but we may not have the ability, the money, or the time. We may not even be interested in that level of presentation.

So instead of overwhelming ourselves with such a feat, let's start small with a story. Add to that story another family story. Build a collection of all the stories we know and then gather as many as we can from others—stories that will help us learn, grow, laugh, find courage, or find peace in our current circumstances. If we gather stories, they will belong to us, and we will belong to our large, extended family.

Someday your descendants may be telling your stories. Someday your story may save a family member in their time of need or trial.

Let's start small. Let's start easy. Share stories. Gather stories. Repeat. These interactions with our living families will build enduring bonds within our entire family: past, present, and future generations.

My invitation to you is to start thinking of your family history as more than a tree; it's a story. And it's time to play with it. Play with it every day in some way.

WISDOM: Work with what you have and share it with the people you love.

2

FABLES

a fable is a short story with a moral or a lesson. They are often humorous. The main characters are typically animals, but not always.

Aesop is credited with hundreds of fables that began with the oral tradition of storytelling. Centuries later they were collected in written form. Some of the more common are "The Tortoise and the Hare," "The Goose that Laid the Golden Eggs," "The Lion and the Mouse," "The North Wind and the Sun," and "The Milkmaid and Pail."

Aesop started telling fables 600 years BC and they were good enough that for hundreds of years afterward he was still being credited with the stories. Aristotle wrote *Rhetoric* about 350 BC and mentions Aesop's fables. That was nearly three hundred years later! I would love to tell stories that would be told for the next twenty-five hundred years! Wouldn't you?

And mMaybe we can. Let's look at why Aesop's fables are so well-remembered.

The purpose of Aristotle's *Rhetoric* was to discuss the theory and action of persuasion by using examples. Since he used Aesop as part of that thought process, he offered that a fable was to persuade the listener or reader to a certain point of view or proof that a certain point of view has merit. In essence, Aristotle explained the importance of fables and that fables represent persuasive speaking or writing. They are events that have happened before or invented examples used as a teaching technique.

Aesop had the right idea: Tell a short story to persuasively teach a concept or lesson. While doing so, ingrain the audience with a catchphrase that will stay with the person and fortify the lesson. Make sure the story is fun and entertaining. You can even have several versions of the story to help get the point across.

I can imagine Aesop starting out by telling his fables as bedtime stories and finding them working on his children. Maybe he progressed to telling his fables to coworkers, friends, and community. Can you see him preparing a lecture to his students or audience and thinking, "I need to start off with a story"? Twenty-first century marketing doesn't have anything groundbreaking in their advice of telling a story before you present your topic or product. It's an attention getter. It is a way to get the buy-in or an agreed need for a product or point of view.

Why did your Aunt Maggie always say, "Don't count your chickens before they are hatched"? Can we guess she had chickens we never knew about? Maybe. Or maybe she heard a story so powerful and meaningful that she incorporated it into her own narrative. It had lasting impact for her. The story was so powerful that 2500 years after Aesop, Aunt Maggie told it to her nieces in one single sentence, and we were expected to know exactly what she meant. The fable goes generally like this:

"The Milkmaid and Pail"

A country maid was walking along with her milk can on top of her head when she began to daydream about all the money she could make when she sold her milk. She would buy eggs which would hatch into chickens. She would take the chickens to market to sell and buy a beautiful dress to wear to the fair. There all the boys would want to dance with her, but she would refuse them all! Completely lost in thought, the country maid shook her head violently to tell them no! The deep thought passed from her imagination into action and down came the can of milk and all was gone.

The moral? Don't count your chickens before they are hatched.

Now, this is just a story. A fable. But for imagination's sake, let's pretend that this is a true story told 2500 years ago in a family setting. A mother, Jane, sends her daughter Mary to the market with her best can of milk and tells her that she can have all the money she sells it for. Mary is delighted. After all, this is her first opportunity to earn a little money. Off Mary goes to the market to sell her milk, carrying the can of milk on top of her head like her mother taught her. Et cetera. It all happens to her, and she returns home and tells her mother the sad story. Her mother exclaims, "Mary, you got carried away with yourself and your daydreams. You should have been concentrating on getting to the market, not counting your chickens before they were hatched."

Yes, it was a life lesson for Mary, and years later she finds herself giving her own daughter a big chore to accomplish. She sets Lily down and tells her, "Let me tell you a story of a little country maid that walked to the market with a can of milk upon her head . . ." The child giggles at the foolish maid and understands the moral and lesson of the story. "Was it you, Mother?" Mary confesses it was, and they have a wonderful talk about what happened next so many years ago. The little girl promises to be careful on her errand the next day. The story could be told for one or two generations before the true names of the family are lost. But it lives on, becoming a fable.

Let's look at another one:

"The Tortoise and the Hare."

A hare teased a tortoise because he was slow and she was fast. The tortoise just laughed and said, "I will challenge you to a race, and we shall see." The race was agreed upon, and all the other animals gathered to watch. Off went the start of the race, and the tortoise stepped off slow and steady with the end in mind. The hare, overconfident that she'd beat the slow tortoise, took the matter lightly as she raced toward the finish line. Just before the finish line, she saw how far back the tortoise still was and decided to mock him by taking a nap and causing greater humiliation for the tortoise. Meanwhile the tortoise plodded on, passed by the sleeping hare, and arrived at the finish line to the cheer of all that watched. The cheering woke up the hare. She was surprised she had lost.

Moral of the story: Slow and steady wins the race.

That one line is all we have to say today. Our minds fill in the blank with the whole story and we nod our heads in agreement.

Now, what if the story was based on a real family? Perhaps the original story is about George who was a little slow, or short, or young compared to others, and his parents told him over and over that slow but sure wins the race. If he put his mind to the task at hand, he could finish anything. George is confronted by a peer that thinks they are faster and better than him and mocks his weaknesses in some way. George thinks of the lessons his parents have taught him and, by applying those lessons, he finds that he can beat the faster, stronger, more confident peer if he just applies himself. It is a lesson George learned early and benefited from for years to come.

Now, as an old grandpa, he is trying to entertain his grand-children one night around the fire and says, "Let me tell you a story of a tortoise and a hare." The children are entertained, the lesson is clear, and grandpa just shared his family history without naming himself as the tortoise. But what a great way to end the story! When grandpa says, "And I was the tortoise!" his grandchildren cheer. They beg him to retell the story night after night, and they in turn tell it to their children years later. Grandpa George and his name are lost in time, but the powerful family story lives on as a fable, with animals in the starring role.

Let's look at another example. Who doesn't remember the fable of "The Boy Who Cried Wolf"? Have you told or read the full story to your children, grandchildren, nieces, or nephews? If you just said at the dinner table tonight "don't be the boy who cried wolf," would everyone at the table instantly know the story and understand what you meant?

If this newest generation hasn't heard these fables, we can retell them to share life's lessons and values. We should tell "The Boy Who Cried Wolf" when we catch our younger ones (teenagers too) in a lie. Teach the lesson that a shepherd boy once learned after lying. While tending the sheep, he would sometimes for fun call "Wolf! Wolf!" and watch the village people run to the field to help him save the sheep. After a time or two, they were tired and weary and angry at the boy's lies. One night, the wolf did indeed come into the field, and the boy called, "Wolf! Wolf!" But no one came, and the wolf devoured the sheep. The boy learned too late that liars are not believed even when they tell the truth. Don't be like the boy who cried wolf.

It can often be easier and more effective to discuss a person's bad habit in the abstract—like a fable—rather than directly. Let's say you have a child that wakes up sick every day and claims they cannot go to school. You know they are not sick every day, and you tell your child the fable of "The Boy Who Cried Wolf." Now you ask your child, "Do you understand the connection?" They do. They understand that, if they keep lying about being sick, no one will believe them when they really are sick. They self-learn the concept because of the simple but powerful story.

Telling this fable to your child could open a discussion on the importance of telling the truth. You could share a lie you once told and what the consequences were. Or you could share a time that something good came from telling the truth, and you were believed because you were trusted as a truth teller. Lessons like these are ones that our family members, both young and old, can learn from and cherish.

The point is that a short, concise story can have incredible power in our family's lives. And our own family stories are just as powerful as any of Aesop's fables. So take a family story and turn it into something fun you can share! Turn it into a fable. Tell the same story many times in different ways, as a true story and as a fable. The hope is that our family members can develop their own memorable catch phrases—phrases that they will pull out in times of decision, reflection, or need. Our family stories and our personal stories have the power to change and strengthen our loved ones. We should be finding life lessons and morals in our family's lives and sharing them.

ACTION ITEM: Remember a few times in your life when you learned a valuable lesson. Write the story down as it actually happened, then write down your story in fable form (perhaps changing the characters into animals), then write down the moral or lesson (how learning that made a difference to you). In just a few sentences, write the story down as it actually happened. Now see if you can fashion it like a fable. Can you change the characters into animals? Can you come up with a catch phrase that summarizes the moral or lesson you learned? How did learning that make a difference to you? Aesop would be so proud of you! Now go find a family member to tell the story to.

SHARING OUR PICTURES

I always teach that we don't own our ancestors! Please try to see the shared humanity in our ancestor's photos. Be generous with your living relatives, no matter how distant, by sharing ancestor pictures.

There is an expression that you can't miss what you never had. Wrong! I was only a baby when my Great Grandmother Lary died. I feel cheated that I didn't know her. But at the very least, I had some photos of her. She was born in 1873, and there is one picture of her as a toddler. There is one wedding photo from 1892. There are maybe a handful of pictures of her as an adult. What if I wasn't the family member to possess them? She had nine children and only one could take physical possession of those few precious photos. I would never be content knowing a wedding picture of her existed but resided with a distant cousin who would not share it. I'd want to see it. I'd want to know what she looked like.

Luckily, I am the one with the wedding photo and the other photos. So now the shoe is on the other foot! Since I would want those photos shared with me, how could I not share? The first time I was shown her wedding photo, I was profoundly shocked that I was looking at a mirror image of myself. Yes, it was a paper picture, but it reflected my face in every way. My grandmother let me see it, but I had to wait decades to have my own copy. I still treasure it today, especially as it began my love of genealogy.

Think of the lasting good you can do for relatives just by sharing the photos you have. They may not even know what they were missing until suddenly it is there before their eyes. And they are captivated and transformed by the experience. Whatever desire they already had to have a connection or relationship with their ancestors will deepen. That's the power of family photos.

Our many-times-great grandparents may have taken only a handful of pictures in their lifetime. It wasn't like they could do reprints, make multiple copies with copy machines, or electronically scan them. Instead, one person was lucky enough to inherit the only photos that existed and "own" them. Does this mean that all the other family members don't get to have a copy for themselves? Yes, the family member physically owns the original photo. But the picture of the person belongs to all the posterity. The absolutely amazing thing is that every member of the family *can* see with their own eyes the faces of our shared ancestors, thanks to the internet. We can copy and upload these images so that everyone can have a picture of great grandmother and great grandfather!

If the thought of sharing all the family photos feels like an overwhelming ordeal, or you're not sure where to start, let me share three free and easy steps.

Let's start with free! Let's keep it easy!

1: Make Digital Copies of Your Photos

Step one is to make a digital copy of each family photo. There are at least three ways you can go about this:

a) Use a smartphone to take pictures of each photo. Then, upload them to a computer or cloud service. If you don't personally have a smartphone, find someone with one and enlist them to help.

b) Use a scanner to scan each photo and save them to a computer or "cloud" computer file storage service. Again, if you don't have a scanner, you can find a relative or friend who does.

c) Find a Family History Center. Most of the Family History Centers in North America offer a free scanner for public use. You can upload/save the photos to a flash drive and take them home with you, or you can scan them all into your free FamilySearch gallery (a cloud service) and work with them later when you get home. All you have to do is walk into the Family History Center with your pictures and thumb drive; a volunteer will be there to get you started. To find a Family History Center nearest you, go to this link: familysearch.org/help/fh-centers/locations. Put in your zip code in the search field. You'll find the addresses of the centers closest to you, along with the phone number, hours of operation, and website.

And there you have it: three free and easy ways to digitize your family photos. Make it even easier by getting others involved. If a relative asks you what you want for your birthday, anniversary, or holiday present, tell them to gift their time and scan all your photos. Or offer to pay your family member by the hour or per picture. Paying your family for their help still follows this easy method and is just a small step up from free.

Let me tell you how I got my family involved in digitizing my photos. Several years ago, I invited my adult daughters over for a digitizing party. I asked them to bring their computer and scanner over to my house. We set up a table, and I divided the family photos into piles for the girls. Did I get perfectly scanned images? No, afterward I had a few photos that were missing some of the top or bottom or the quality wasn't great. But the job was done! I could go back through as I named the files and scan again those few outliers. We had a whole day of fun being together, talking some about family history and stories, but mostly just enjoying the conversations of our current lives.

Recently, I found about a hundred photos that had never been scanned. I set up the scanner and the process. My twelve year old grandson came over and I asked for his help. Parker loves family history, loves technology, and enjoys having some-thing to do when he comes over with his family. He sat in the room with the adults and scanned those hundred photos and got to listen in to all our conversation while scanning. I call that a big win. He was serving the past, listening to the present, and preparing for a future with confidence in tech-nology and family history. Plus, he now knows how to go to his other grandparents' home and scan the other side of the family's photos.

Now let's get technical with our first step. You'll want to make the request or choose for yourself that your photos are saved as a TIFF or JPEG.

What is the difference between the two file types? TIFF files maintain the highest quality for future uses, even after edit-ing. These high quality files are used commercially and professionally. The downside is that TIFF files are large and take up lots of room. For this reason, saving images as a JPEG is more common. It's the standard, or default, choice of the average digital phone or camera. JPEG compresses the file so it does not take up too much memory, but you could have data loss (such as blurred faces or handwritten text upon the original photo) as you change sizes of the photo. JPEGS are high quality but not the best quality.

I have sat in so many genealogical classes where the photo archival experts admonish us to save in TIFF. They say that we did it all wrong if we saved in JPEG. You can hear the audience sigh in great sorrow that they did it "wrong" as a "novice" mistake. But JPEG is a good choice; don't let the experts make you cry over it. Save your photos as TIFF files if you can but save it in JPEG if space is an issue. File type is important but not more important than getting it done free and easy. I would rather have a poor copy or even a paper copy than no photo at all. A good compromise is to scan the most important pictures in TIFF format and the others in JPEG.

2. Name Your Photos

When all the photos are in the computer, give them each a name. You do this by right clicking on the photo. Then, choose "Rename" to give the file a name. Alternatively, instead of a quick double click on the file (which would open the file), you may click once, wait a few moments, then click a second time. Then type what you wish to name the photo.

There are all kinds of naming systems and lots of people telling you how to do it "right." There are pros and cons to every naming system. The important thing is that you name them. You might search the internet for different file naming conventions to get an idea of your options. For example, you can start with the ancestor's last name, first name, and year the photo was taken. Or maybe you want to name the file with the year first, then the name.

If you only have one person in the photo, it's easy to name it "1890 Traci Gormley in Texas." It's easy to name a two-person photo as "1890 John Smith and Traci Gormley Smith marriage in Texas." But what do you do if you pick up the next photo and you have ten people pictured there? What if you don't know the date or the names? This is where all those naming systems either make your life easy or give you a headache. When picking a naming system, think about how you are most likely to sort your photos when looking for a particular picture. Are you going to sort by name or date?

WARNING: Some people just name each image with a number. They create a separate document that lists the picture numbers with complete descriptions of the photos. They might even include the story behind the picture within the document. Although this sounds like a great way to organize and share family photos, if the photos get separated from the list, the next generation is left with photos of unknown relatives. The family history is lost.

Yet, I know why people do this! You want to record everything about the photo, but it is sometimes impossible to capture all the background story and details all within a file name. Try to name the picture as thoroughly as you can. Give the date. Name the people and the place. Then, if you have more information to share, write everything you know about the picture down on a piece of paper. Or type the information and print it out. You can scan that piece of paper with the picture as one image file. With the picture and writing scanned together, you ensure that the vital information is preserved.

When it comes to naming your family photos, just getting it done is the most important thing, not only for personally finding the photos, but also for helping future generations quickly identify the who, when and where. You can always tweak the file names later.

3. Share Your Photos

Your photos now are labeled with some sort of name in the computer (or phone). If you had a friend do this on their computer, they can put the files on a flash drive for easy transfer onto your computer. Once it is on your computer, you are ready for step three: Share your photos!

How do you want to do this? Pick the method that works for you or for that friend or family member sitting beside you. Here are some ideas:

You can upload your pictures one at a time to the top genealogy sites like Ancestry, FamilySearch, and My Heritage. These sites allow you to attach each picture directly to individual ancestors. This will take some time, but remember that you can do this little by little. Slow and steady wins the race! Upload even just one family photo, and now you are sharing with strangers who are actually related to you in some magical way. I'm sure that your distant relatives will feel similar to me when they see your pictures; I thrill at finding a picture of an ancestor on one of these sites. It's better than a Christmas present.

What are some other ways you can share your photos? You can upload them to Facebook or another social media plat-form. Sharing in this way with living family members will spark memories, inspire questions, and start conversations. You might even have a family member reshare your post.

You can upload your photos to any cloud service you have: your phone cloud service, Google Photos, Amazon Photo, and so on. There are dozens of cloud storage services for free. Ask someone who knows your computer software if you might have free cloud storage that you don't know about. Once you've uploaded your photos onto your cloud service, give your family access so they can have all the photos. Alternatively, you could download them onto flash drives for your family to put on their computers.

Please know this is the bare bones way to share your family photos. Anyone can do it! If this is the best and only thing you do with your photos, it is so much better than nothing. I hope you have the confidence that you *can* do it—free and easy.

If you'd like to put more effort into sharing and really have some fun, find ways to play with the pictures you have. It costs almost nothing to make a few paper copies and play pin the mustache on great grandpa. Have some fun with sharing your photos!

- Cut copies of your photos into puzzle pieces, and let children reassemble.
- Make stick puppets by taping a family picture to a ruler or popsicle stick. Then, tell bedtime stories and teach children the family names to call each puppet they can use in their play with the stick puppets.

- Cut two or more copies of pictures and see if kids can put them together separating two different pictures cut and mixed together.
- Put a map on the wall and let kids discover where each person was born and have them label it.
- Send a picture out in your family group text and watch a conversation develop over memories, questions, comments. I often do this with my siblings, and it brings us together as we talk about our shared story.

If you are thinking you have a little more money to throw at preserving and sharing your photos, you can purchase dozens of different types and brands of scanners to scan your photos all in the comfort of your own home. There are also different types and prices of cloud storage accounts where you can upload your pictures.

You can even box up your photos and mail them to a professional for them to scan and file. Then they can give you access to the digital files. If you want to go this route, be brave enough to ask all your family to participate by chipping in some of the money. Even if the price tag is large, dividing with everyone getting access may be the way you want to go.

I hope you feel a sense of excitement in digitizing, naming, and sharing your family's photos. It can be as free and easy as you make it. It really is a fun and easy process that you repeat over and over again. It only costs your time once you know what you're doing and get into the rhythm of doing it.

Labeling or naming your pictures gets easier too, and you will find what works best for you.

If you will see this as a loving service to your ancestors and as a loving service to present and future generations, you will feel an abundant joy. Your relatives will see the family photos you've shared and will love and appreciate your efforts. I think of this as a gift to all present and future family.

ACTION ITEM: After you get the spirit of digitizing your own photos, go to a loved one's home that has family pictures hanging on the wall. First, take a photo of their framed picture. Then, have them hold a picture while you take a photo of them holding it. Ask them to tell you a story about the picture. When you leave, you will have a wonderful piece of family story.

4

FAMILY STORIES LIGHT OUR WAY

The ideals which have lighted me on my way, and time after time given me new courage to face life cheerfully, have been Goodness, Beauty, and Truth.

—Albert Einstein, *The World As I See It*

I can litter a hallway floor with lots of things and have you walk it in the dark. You will step on things. You will kick things. You may even trip over things and want to give up. But if I turn on the light and you can see clearly, you will navigate the hallway with confidence! Light has a way of eliminating our fear and discouragement. Our personal and family stories can be such a light for us. As we remember these stories in our everyday lives, we let them light our way, giving us insight, confidence, and courage to move through our daily choices.

How do we let our family stories light the way?

If your ancestors crossed an ocean and started life in a new land, our children, knowing that fact only or a more detailed story, may find the courage to cross their oceans of change and their new beginnings. The experiences do not need to be the same for the lesson to be applied and the loneliness of the journey diminished.

Let's say that your relative is nervous about moving far away for school or a new job. How simple it is to make a comparison to one of their ancestors! Telling the story of when an ancestor went through something similar can both teach them and offer them confidence in their abilities to succeed.

"You know, one of your great-grandmothers, Temperance Flowerdew, was an early settler of Jamestown before America was America! In 1609, she sailed on the ship *Falcon* to come here. She survived the 'Starving Time' and ended up one of the wealthiest women in Virginia before she died in 1628. The starving time killed 80% of the Jamestown settlers but not our grandmother! Did you know she survived a hurricane on one of her ocean trips? She also ate rats for dinner. If she can do it, you can do it! You have her DNA in you!"

Your pep talk could include a follow-up. Give your family member a little biography about Temperance or tell them to look her up on the internet and read more about her. It may just light the way for your relative, giving them courage to face their own larger-than-life challenges.

Let's say a child (your child, grandchild, niece, or nephew) is afraid to go to elementary school, junior high, or high school. Imagine giving them your Temperance Flowerdew pep talk.

That child is going to say, "She ate *rats*!" That will stick with them. They don't have it so bad they have to eat rats. "She was in a hurricane!" That is one tough ancestor. The story of the conquering Temperance Flowerdew lights the way for the present descendent to move forward in their own life with a sense of *I can do this*.

Let's look at something interesting about the Einstein quote at the beginning of this chapter. He mentions an emotion. I love that something lights his way (very visual) but also that it evokes an emotion. I enjoy that Einstein also said the ideals that lighted his way gave him the ability to face life cheerfully.

Cheerfully.

Life can be short or long; it can go by slow or fast. It can be boring or exciting, and it can be hard or easy. Life mixes everything up but often not evenly. We can have a series of bad luck or a long run of easy. We can carry a burden in our heart or mind for months or years at a time. As we move through our days, months, and years, how do we *face* life? Can we face life cheerfully, embrace whatever comes our way, and see the best that can be seen?

Let's consider that Einstein said the *ideals* are what lit his way. What is an ideal? It is a very lofty word meaning something that is perfection. An ideal is the highest standard or model of excellence. An ideal is the highest goal and the ultimate desire of our hearts. The highest goals and desires for Einstein were goodness, beauty, and truth. These are the ideals that we want to capture in our family stories! We want to let these ideals light the way for the present. We can find these meaningful family stories two ways: 1) we can think of the family story first and then find the ideal that it shares, or 2) we can make a list of ideals and try to remember a family story that will teach that ideal.

Think of a personal or family story. Now, what is the meaning, message, or life lesson of the story? Can you reframe it, so it has purpose to someone that you love today? Stories that seem to have no purpose can suddenly become meaningful. A humorous story may show us by example to have a good attitude or be a good sport. That lesson can light the way for a present-day family member to internalize that attribute. A story of grief can give someone permission to grieve themselves but then continue on to live a purposeful life. Your own story of embarrassment or failing can be a testimony that it isn't fatal, that it passes, and that better days do reappear.

Now, instead of thinking of the story first, think of an *ideal* you would like your family to learn. Remember an ideal is perfection, the goal, or the highest role model. It's what you hope for your family. Do you have personal or family stories that can teach toward the ideal? What were the three things Einstein picked for himself? Truth, goodness, and beauty.

What words would you choose to face life cheerfully? What experiences have you had that would be an example for others that would light their way?

What words would you choose for family members if you were naming each other's best traits? How did they get those traits? (There is a story.)

Even relatives that seem to have no positive traits can still have stories that teach us ideals. I can think of a family member that I can fit in that mold. It may be tempting to teach "don't be like Uncle Bob." But that's horrible. The whole purpose of family history is to unite and uplift our family members! So is there a way to turn their stories around and still teach our ideals? If you can, include this person in your storytelling. Reach out to this Uncle Bob and invite him to tell you some stories of his life and what he learned. He may surprise you and the whole family. He may have positive traits and experiences you were not aware of. You may understand why he is the way he is and be able to find mercy or compassion. This exercise can bring healing for the whole family. Maybe if you begin to share the family's stories, you will see a change in even Uncle Bob. You can be a light upon their way of change and growth.

A good time to learn and share family stories are around funeral events. It can be a healing time where we cry and laugh and remember family members. In my experience, we gather as a family for a big dinner after the funeral, and before long, people are telling stories about the family and the deceased. These stories bring more tears and lots of laughter. These stories are true and honest and burn within us remembrances of our loved one. We can talk of their goodness, their personality, their experiences that made them a beautiful person. It doesn't matter what kind of character they were. Accepting them for what they are, we can see they were a beautiful person in our family. Even the "worst" person in our family has taught us lessons we live by.

As we laugh and cry together, the grief is soothed in the smallest measure, healing may begin, and the memories we have shared linger in our minds and hearts for days. We should capture those stories told at funerals and family gatherings. We don't naturally go into a grieving family experience with the forethought of "gather family stories!" but perhaps we should. We should quietly write them down during or immediately after. We should ask a few follow-up questions to get a better, complete story.

Even though I never knew my great-grandfather William Texas Gooch, I like him and "remember" him in a way. I understand his personality, in part, because I have small insights into his parents and the time period in which he lived. I have several pictures of him that let my mind and heart "see" him. My mother has many loving memories of her grandfather and has shared them with me. They have become my memories although not from my personal experience. She tells one interesting tidbit that tells me a lot about his personality: He loved to debate. He would take a side and debate it to death with someone. But the very next day, he would take the other side of the argument and debate it with the next person.

At his funeral, the preacher said something that summed up this personality: "Mr. Gooch had strong opinions, and I liked him for it." Notice the preacher didn't say he agreed. As small snippets of his life and personality have been shared,

Grandpa William becomes real to me. I feel connected to him.

I have learned that our relationships are not over when someone dies. It only changes form. *The connection is the relationship*. We accept this readily in living relationships. We have relationships where we see a person every day, weekly, monthly, annually, or once a decade. We have face-to-face relationships, as well as relationships over phone, text, letters, and social media. We still have relationships with long-lost schoolmates that made a difference in our lives. Do you have a friend that you haven't seen for months or years but, at your very greeting, all the years melt away and it is just the same as it was? It is the feeling of connection, a shared association, and the quality of the connection with someone that is the essence of the relationship.

Our relationships with deceased loved ones are the same. We still have our feelings for them. We can remember their lives, their stories, and the love they had for their family. We can hold their picture and see their faces again. We can listen to a recording and hear their voices again. We can hold their favorite pipe, necklace, or toy that they held and feel a connection to them.

I remember the first time I found my great grandfather's grave in the little town of Carlton, Texas. On the tombstone it read: "To live in hearts we leave behind is not to die." I was just a young girl then, but I pondered it for days and weeks. When I was older, I went looking for the quote and found it in Thomas Campbell's (1777–1844) poem "Hallowed

Ground." I love that poem. I love the question he asks, "But where's their memory's mansion? Is't Yon churchyard's bowers? No! in ourselves their souls exist, a part of ours."

Whether you believe in the idea of a soul or not, it is at least absolutely true that their DNA exists, a part of ours! Our ancestors are a forever part of us.

Where is our ancestor's memory mansion? It is in our minds and hearts and the stories we tell about them. Think back to the earlier statement by Einstein that ideals (think stories) can light the memory mansions of people. Write your own stories so others will find the light you leave for them. Write your ancestors' stories so we can learn attributes and character traits that will bring light to our eyes and emulate and encourage others. Write your own children's experiences so they will have recorded for them some of their defining moments illuminated beautifully by your hand.

We can look for, remember, record, and retell stories in our family circles to provide the light to help someone navigate their daily world. Everyone goes through bad times or even wandering times. If we share stories of truth, goodness, beauty, hope, encouragement, and humor, these same stories will come into our memories again and again and provide us cheerfulness to endure and hold on. Our stories can provide the next generation with the fortitude of our ancestors.

It is a process: We need to learn and know our family's stories and keep them in our hearts. We also need to write them down and share them with our family so they too may benefit from their ancestral ideals.

ACTION ITEM: Pick a deceased or living relative that you personally know or knew. Do a brain dump of everything you can remember about them. Just make a list on paper, listing anything and everything you can think of this family member. Add every story even if it is super short. Then, go into your genealogy research and photo albums and gather any information you have there. Once your list is created, now add to it how you *felt* about the person. Did you learn anything from them? Were you happy to see them? Do you admire them for any reason? Do you do something today because of them? Maybe they taught you a life hack like how to scoop fat off soup with a piece of bread, or maybe you now use a saying or a phrase that was once theirs. Fix up this information however you want and share this family member's story.

ADDED BONUS: When you send out an all-points bulletin to all your family about the relative, tell them you are gathering everything about Aunt or Uncle or Grandpa or Grandma. Ask them to do a brain dump of the person too and send it to you. Or invite everyone over to a family dinner and do this action item together, appointing a couple of scribes to take notes. What a fun family activity of remembering, collecting, and sharing!

ADDED, ADDED BONUS: Does anyone have something that belonged to this person? Take a picture of it, and then describe the item and how it relates to the person. Make the connection with items they loved, treasured, passed down, or left behind.

5

EXPRESSIONS WE SAY

*W*ho knew that we have family members (past or present) that through their oft-used expressions gave guidance, advice, or opinions? Expressions, coaching, and idioms all are shortcut helps we use to encourage others to achieve their best self.

Our ancestors, grandparents, parents, teachers, and mentors often quoted, taught, or lived by phrases that provided deeper meaning and direction for our own lives. We received a life's lesson or cautionary advice that kept us on a good path. Short phrases can pack a punch.

With more than 25,000 expressions out there in English alone, we can glean thousands of life's lessons from them! Idioms such as:

- Bloom where you're planted.
- It's a piece of cake.

- It's raining cats and dogs.
- Let me be the devil's advocate.
- All is fair in love and war.
- Add insult to injury.
- Kill two birds with one stone.
- He could spin a yarn.
- No use crying over spilled milk.
- To bite the bullet.

Shakespeare used expressions to give depth, perspective, and understanding in his plays. Some of Shakespeare's include:

- Heart of gold (*Henry V*)
- Kill with kindness (*Taming of the Shrew)*
- A charmed life (*Macbeth*)
- Send him packing (*Henry IV*)
- Run the wild goose chase (*Romeo and Juliet*)
- It is the green-eyed monster (*Othello*)

Do you have family members that used common phrases or expressions that conveyed meaning? Did they have favorite phrases they applied to various situations? These would make great stories to remember and to share with others. It speaks to the person's outlook on life or shows how they attempted to comfort, teach, or encourage their family and friends.

Do *you* use idioms or expressions? Write them down and tell why and how you use them or how they help others. Where did you pick up your expressions?

As a fun activity, you can search "idioms" on the internet and find your own new motto for your life. Find a few you would like to foster and build upon and use the idiom in your conversations to illustrate the principle with a family story. Tell it to your children.

Short expressions allow us to grab the real issue and face it head on. No lecture. It gets to the point. When our families or friends tell us about a challenge they are going through, an expression may lighten the mood, and the catchphrase is remembered. These expressions can bolster your loved one's confidence to go forward and walk through the test or trial. Think of the little train, "I think I can."

I am not saying to be trite in our conversations, but ponder on the expressive language of the family members you know. See if you can pull out of your memory or your every day how you and others around you give advice. Then, capture that in a short snippet or story.

You may find the perfect phrases to help your own family and friends. "Granddad Smith told his girls that it was better to send them packing rather than to marry and regret." What's the story behind that one? Now when someone in the family responds "send them packing," it also means to take action now rather than regret a choice later. Expressions can take on new, deeper meanings within the family setting.

The same can be said for movie quotes, Bible quotes, quotes from famous people. Search your memory and ask other living family members what their favorite quotes, phrases, or idioms are and why. No one will even suspect you are building a family story book or a birthday or Christmas present. Wouldn't you love to get a quote book that shares favorite quotes from each member of the family and explains *why* it is their favorite? It's a small and simple thing that can give us a connection and build bridges of understanding and appreciation.

How comforting it is and how simple to share a family member's words. "Your mother always said . . ." or "Your uncle always said . . ."

Some of the quotes may be stories or songs that have been told and retold in the family. For example, my father told a short, lively story of "Pay the Rent." It was a skit where, as he used different character's voices, he would move a bow tie around. He would put the bow on the top of the head when the girl spoke, under his nose like a mustache for the villain and at the base of his neck for the hero. As little children, my siblings and I loved that skit and for years cheered for encore performances. He told it to us dozens of times. He told it to our children dozens of times. It is a wonderful memory, and we retell it again when we sit around and remember him together. It isn't an original skit. Some say it is from the earliest vaudeville days. My father first heard it in the 1951 movie *Westward the Women.* He was twelve when he saw it in the movie theater—which takes me to another strong memory of him loving old cowboy movies. Of course, they weren't old the first time he watched them. But as he watched them again and again with his children and grand-children, we grew to love cowboy movies too. The "Pay the Rent" skit is now a part of our family story.

Oft-repeated phrases can also become part of family remembrances. My mother, after eighty years, still spells geography using a statement she learned in grade school. "Geography: George ate an old gray rat at Paul's house yesterday."

Songs can become a part of the family's history just as easy. Does your family have a theme song? Does a family member have a song they learned as a child that even thirty, fifty, seventy years later they can sing word-perfectly? Ask your ninety-year-old relative her favorite childhood song and see if she breaks into singing. Many adults now can sing along with Joe Raposo's 1969 hit "Can You Tell Me How to Get to Sesame Street" or "Over the Rainbow" made famous by Judy Garland in *The Wizard of Oz*. My children know the correct planet order by singing "The Planet Song" they learned watching *Blue's Clues* on television. We need those songs in our family's history.

Maybe it's not a saying, quote, or song that is stuck in your family's history. Could it be a jingle that is front and center in your family folklore? Generations of people can finish these jingles.

Plop, plop, fizz, fizz . . .

It takes a licking and keeps on . . .

I wish I was an Oscar Meyer wiener . . .

The best part of waking up . . .

I'd like to teach the world to sing . . .

.   .   .

See the possible power in even the shortest idioms, phrases, expressions, stories, and songs? They can last a lifetime—multiple lifetimes—in our memories. Before indelibly imbedding something into your family, first make sure that it can help with positive feelings, motivations, or memories. Then, record it and share it with everyone.

My nephew, a Boy Scout, was on a mountain climbing hike that became much too hard for him. In this moment, his mind turned to his grandpa, a man who loved scouting. He thought of his grandpa's jokes and songs, and the memories of those things suddenly encouraged him. It was the happy memories of his scouting grandfather that propelled him forward with new determination and strength. Wow! This is a wonderful example of family history stories making a difference in our lives and in the lives of our grandchildren and beyond.

Notice the connection: The grandfather has a good living relationship with a young grandson. They sang songs and told jokes and stories for fun. Several years later, the young grandson calls upon the relationship and memory of his grandfather's interaction, enabling him to accomplish a hard mountain hike. The grandfather blesses the grandson in two ways: fun in the moment and courage in the future trial. The grandson enjoys the interaction with his grandfather in jokes, songs and stories and later draws upon that to help him complete a task when he is starting to lose confidence in his abilities. Can you see the reciprocal relationship between generations? Can you see the value of sharing stories to coach family members through life's experience?

Congratulations, you are also participating in life training, as you learn to help your family maximize their time, talent, energy, attitude, motivation, and communication. You do this by providing them with short, helpful stories that they can ponder and incorporate into their lives.

How fun it will be when you collect up everyone's favorite idioms, maxims, expressions, songs, poems, stories, and jokes, and make a list! When your family gets together next, you can say, "Let's play a game." You'll pull out the best get-to-know-you game that there is. You'll get to know each other in a new way. If you don't want to collect people's favorite words through a game, it's also a conversation starter. When I ask, "Who in the family can spell geography?" not only does my mother become known to her family in a new and different way, but she can elaborate on what she remembers, who was the teacher, how old she was, and other facts about school. When I ask, "Who can say the planets in the correct order?" four of my seven children will start to sing and enjoy sibling camaraderie and relive those childhood days of happiness.

Every person has something from their life—a saying, a quote, or a song—that brings back dozens of memories. Remembering these expressions from a relative's life and finding the stories behind them can be a fun game to play. Recording them preserves forever an important part of your relative's personality. And sharing these expressions out gives the entire family insight and understanding. As we remember our relatives' favorite words and the stories behind them, we can draw on our own family history to make good choices and have confidence in our future success.

ACTION ITEM:

Ask people questions such as:

"Do you remember going to the ball games (fishing, mowing the yard) with Dad?"

"Do you remember the kinds of meals your mother made?"

"Do you remember what your grandma used to always say?"

"Do you remember summers at your grandparents' house?"

"Did your (family member) ever give you advice?"

"Do you remember the last visit with (family member)?"

6

ASK AND ASK AGAIN

*B*efore we can share our family stories, the first step is to capture them. I've seen that it's often the *questions* we ask that help us bring out and capture these stories.

Some questions are more effective than others at inviting storytelling, with some of the best questions opening the door to many more. Family history websites and other online resources have hundreds upon hundreds of great questions you can ask your family members. You will also find a list of questions in the next chapter. You can ask these questions interview style or send them to your relative as a question-naire. Sending them questions gives them a way to write out their own life story.

Questions do not ensure that we'll get the perfect or most complete history within the responses; there aren't enough questions we could ask our oldest generation, but you have to start and stop somewhere. Pick some questions, and arrange them either chronologically or thematically. This way, when you record all the answers in order, you'll have a nice flow. After reading all the responses, fill in any gaps you see by asking follow-up questions!

While I was away at college and taking my first family history class, I sent a list of questions to my grandparents. My grandfather was a newspaperman, so he typed up the answers in order, skipping the questions he wanted to skip, and provided me with a pristine, ten-page history for both himself and his wife. It is one of my most prized possessions. I never thought of this at the time, but reading it twenty years later and with them long since passed, I now see places where I should have asked follow-up questions.

For example, my grandmother mentions being raised by her mother, grandmother, and older brother. I should have followed up with "tell me some things about your grandmother!" How did I miss that? She told me all about herself, her mother, and her brother, but not her grandmother. And I didn't ask. I was so happy about getting her ten-page typed story that I didn't even think to go one more step and scrutinize the document for missing information.

Here is another missed opportunity from that same experience. My grandfather told me a lot about his first job and how much he got paid. He then tells me about other jobs he worked, but he never mentions wage. I wish I would have followed up on that. I think especially the men in the family would have been interested that he earned so many cents a day at his first job and then so many dollars a day at his last job before he retired.

Some may not even notice the omission of little details like this. So, after you get their answers, try to proactively think of follow-up questions you could ask. Read each line in their history and ask yourself "What else?" What else is there that you're missing? What more do you need to know to have a more complete history? Then, visit with your family member again, and add to the story.

Sending a list to your family members isn't the only way to present your questions to them. If answering dozens of questions at once seems like too much, you could give them just one question each week. You can send them a question through email or ask them a few questions during a visit. Whether by mail, email, phone call, or text message, it doesn't matter. However they will communicate back with you, *that's* the method you want to choose.

I discovered that my mother, who has basic computer skills, can use the dictation function in email to send me her stories. She can open her email, click on the microphone, speak the question and answer, and then hit send. Her words are automatically transcribed, and I can fix any grammar and punctuation errors. I told her not to worry about that. Just open your email, talk, and send. As older people have more alone time and need things to do, this is a perfect activity for them and a gold mine for their families.

I purchased a small digital recorder (Olympus WS-853) and recorded interviews with my mother while we were on a driving trip. I only needed to give prompting questions and let her talk. We had an enjoyable hour-after-hour conversation. When I came home, I uploaded the digital files to an online transcription service called happyscribe.com. This is state of the art AI (artificial intelligence). It gave an excellent transcription-audio file that I could listen to and read at the same time. Plus, I can edit her stories. It was an easy way to capture oral history and provide a life story to all the other family members.

Again, look at the reciprocal relationship building from this one interaction: Mother and I had a memorable interaction and conversation that was then shared out with all the other family members. They get to enjoy their mother's stories forever. Not only do I have the audio, but I have the transcription. Years from now when she is deceased, my grandchildren and great grandchildren can listen to her voice and read her stories.

I hope this triggers in your mind "yes, and I can do it for my own life stories, and I can tell my children's stories!" How fun it would be for my two-year-old grandchild to grow up and as a teenager listen to me tell one of her funny antics as a child. That is a three generation story right there.

Group Sourcing

To get answers to your questions, remember that the person you are writing about is not the only source you have to turn to. You can group-source a personal history for someone that has passed. Use Facebook, email, or even a text chat for smaller groups. Ask the question as it applies to the person you are building a life story for and let all other living members contribute to the effort. A simple Facebook post with a few questions can get the ball rolling. Week after week, you post a few questions at a time and watch the memories come in response. Then, you become the editor to put it all in one document. Send it out to everyone and ask, "Can you add anything else to this person's story?" You will be surprised that you get additional responses to augment your story.

What if you have a difference of opinion? The difference of opinion could be over a rather trivial fact. For example, Julie believes May's dog was named Spot, but Jeff believes it was Rover. What if Julie believes May favored the boys, but Jeff said May told him once that the boys needed an education because they had to find a living for their future families? Or maybe May said something to her siblings as a youth that she didn't believe in any longer in her late adult years. Capturing the different perspectives of family members helps build a better picture for us. You can include both perspectives in the record and still share a great history.

Even if the family member we're writing about is still alive and well, various perspectives can still help us collect the stories we want and need. My aunt told me once that I didn't know my mother like she knew her. Well, of course. My aunt knew her best as a child, and I didn't know her till she was an adult! If I could have my aunt tell me stories to go along with my mother's and my own, I would have a better story of my mother.

The lesson here? If you're writing your dad's life story, don't bring your questions only to him. Ask other family members for their stories about him! Get your questions list, and ask your living relatives how they think he would answer each question. The memories of your dad's parents, siblings, aunt, uncles, cousins, and grandparents can all work together to build a wonderfully full story.

After recently spending several hours interviewing my own mother for her life story, I was able to get over thirty-five pages of her life story. And that's only covering her childhood and teenage years. I then went on our family Facebook group and announced our start of her story and asked if anyone had any specific questions they wanted included. I got a list of dozens of questions! Many of the answers I knew but had not even noticed the stories were missing. Moral of the story: Ask and ask again!

You can never ask too many questions, and you can never get too many family members involved. As you ask questions, stories will flood back into memory. Capture these stories before it's too late. Capture them in audio recordings and on paper, and share it out! Your family will thank you for it.

ACTION ITEM: Find lists of questions and compile them so you will be ready for the interview process. You may want to ask questions that have one- or two-word answers, as well as open response questions that encourage the person to relate events and details. You may then want to ask questions that require expressing feelings, judgments, thoughts, wishes, or regrets. Depending on when and who you interview, you may need to pace based on their interest or desire to remember.

Ask your older relative the questions.

Write out your answers to those questions.

Ask questions of a group source.

Ask your little children as many questions as apply to them.

7

EXAMPLE QUESTIONS

*I*n chapter 6, we discussed how we can ask questions in order to discover our family stories. But what kinds of questions should we ask? And how do we ask them? This chapter gives you more insight into how you can interview your family members. It also gives you a list of some example questions you can ask them—or yourself, if recording your own personal history. As you look through these questions, notice the flow from one question to the next. Notice that some are short answer, and some require longer answers. Notice that some will give you information and other questions will give you feelings. Try for a mix of questions.

Depending on how much time you and your interviewee have available, you may want to categorize your questions into small groups that you can cover in various interview sessions. Create a group of questions that only pertain to the person's childhood, and tackle those questions on one day. On days to follow, you can tackle their high school years, college years, early married life, and so on. Spreading out your questions gives you a realistic way to cover so much material without exhausting you or your interviewee.

You should also group your interview sessions by who will be the person of focus. If you want the interviewee to talk about themselves and their lives, try to stay focused on them. The next visit, you will ask the same questions, this time about the new person of focus (their parent or sibling, for example). You can have one session where you cover *only* people other than the interviewee themself (grandparents, parents, siblings, children, cousins, and so on). Keeping questions separated like this will help the interview process seem more organized and efficient.

I also believe you should share the questions before you interview so they can have time to think on them. You can reassure them that any question that they want to skip is fine. With the list of questions you have provided to them, your relatives will take the time to think of things they want to share and will prime their memories for it.

So what are some questions you can give them? Below are three different lists of questions you can use. The first list of questions is designed to encourage telling stories from various life stages and events. The second list is designed like a survey; these questions can be answered quickly, usually with one-word answers. You can ask "why?" after any of these questions to get more information. The third list shows various thoughtful questions you can ask. Use these example lists to put together your own questions. You get to decide what questions you ask!

Fifty Story Questions

1. What is your full name? Why did your parents give you that name?
2. When and where were you born? Describe your home, your neighborhood, and the town you grew up in.
3. Tell me about your father (his name, birth date, birthplace, parents, and so on). Can you share some memories you have of your father?
4. Tell me about your mother (her name, birth date, birthplace, parents, and so on). Can you share some memories you have of your mother?
5. What kind of work did your parents do? (For example, were they a farmer, salesman, manager, seamstress, nurse, or stay-at-home mom?)
6. Have any of your family members died yet? If so, what do you remember of their death, and what were the circumstances of their death?
7. What kind of hardships or tragedies did your family experience while you were growing up?
8. What are the names of your brothers and sisters? Describe one or more things that stand out in your mind about each of your siblings.
9. What were some of the family traditions that you remember?

10. Did your family have special ways of celebrating specific holidays?

11. Share a few memories of your grandparents.

12. Did your grandparents live close by? If so, how much were they involved in your life? If they lived far away, did you ever travel to visit them? What was that like?

13. Do you have any aunts, uncles, or cousins who really stand out in your mind? Write something about them. (This could include their name, personalities, events, and stories.)

14. Where did you go to school? What was school like for you?

15. What were your favorite subjects in school? Why?

16. What subjects did you like the least? Why?

17. If you went on to college or vocational education, what school did you go to? What did you study? What are the memories of those years?

18. What do you see as your personal strengths?

19. What were some of the challenges you faced growing up?

20. What medical issues have you had to deal with throughout your life?

21. Was religion an important part of your family life? If so, what religion did your family practice and what did it mean to you? Is it still an important part of your life today? If religion was/is not part of your life, why isn't it?

22. Who were some of your friends in school? What were they like? What happened to them?

23. What foods do you like? Dislike?
24. Were there two or three dishes your mother or father made that make you smile every time you think of them?
25. How did you meet your spouse?
26. Tell me about your spouse (name, birth date, birthplace, parents, and so on). Can you share some memories you have of your spouse?
27. How would you describe your spouse?
28. What was your courtship like?
29. How many children do you have? What are their names? Share a few memories of each child.
30. What were some of the major community, national, or world events you lived through? How did some of these events change your life?
31. What are some of your life philosophies or life views that you would share with other family members?
32. What are some personal values that are important to you? What have you done (or are doing) to teach these values to your children?
33. Think of people throughout the world and throughout time. List at least five people who you would categorize as truly great men or women. What did they do to be great in your mind?
34. List twenty or more things that make you happy.
35. List twenty or more things that you think the world would be so much better off without.
36. List twenty interesting things you've experienced in your lifetime.

37. If you could spend a day with any famous person in the world, who would it be and what would you do during your day with him/her?
38. What scares you?
39. Share a few of the deeply moving (spiritual) experiences you had in your life.
40. What advice would you pass on about raising children that you learned from raising your own children?
41. What are some of your talents? How did you discover them? What have you done to cultivate and improve them?
42. What were some of the truly life changing experiences you went through? How did you handle them? In what ways did they change you?
43. What did you do for a career? Why did you choose to go into this career?
44. What were some of the jobs you had throughout your life? Were there memorable experiences you had with any of those jobs?
45. What would you consider as two or three truly significant challenges in your life so far?
46. What are some of the life lessons that you would like to pass on to your posterity?
47. How many places have you lived? Provide a brief description of each place you've lived and why you lived (or moved) there.
48. If you could go back in time and do things over again, what would you change?
49. When all is said and done, what do you want to be

remembered for? What are you doing now to make
that happen?
50. What were some of your more memorable
vacations?

Survey Questions

1. What are some of your physical traits (like eye color,
hair color, and complexion)?
2. What is your favorite meal, food, drink, and dessert?
3. What is your favorite recipe?
4. What is your favorite color?
5. What is your favorite song?
6. What is your favorite book?
7. What is your favorite movie? TV show?
8. What is your favorite game? Sport? Hobby?
9. What is your favorite pet?
10. What is your favorite zoo animal?
11. What is your favorite holiday?
12. What is your favorite tradition?
13. What is your favorite thing to do?
14. What kind of car do you drive?
15. Do you have special keepsakes?
16. What is your best memory?
17. What would most people not know about you?
18. What famous person, living or dead, would you
want to meet?
19. What is the best piece of advice you have ever been
given?
20. Have you ever had a nickname?

Thoughtful Questions

1. What is your best marriage advice?
2. What is your best parenting advice?
3. How did you overcome regrets, setbacks, disappointments?
4. How did you feel about (some historical moment)?
5. What invention do you most enjoy?
6. What is your most important memory of your parents? Grandparents?
7. What is your favorite memory as a child? As a spouse? As a parent?
8. How do you handle stress?
9. What makes you happy?
10. What makes you sad?
11. How do you feel about politics? Religion? Patriotism? Education?
12. What would you wish for your family?

If the interview process doesn't go as perfectly as you hoped, that's okay! Remember that a person has to be in the mood to respond to certain questions. If they are not in the mood to remember the past, shift the conversation to something more current. If they don't like a question, skip it. And if they get off on a tangent, let them! Why? Because veins of gold run in rock formations, and you are prospecting for the gold among the rock. Allowing others to wander in their answers is not only kind; it is also valuable. You can always bring them back to your list of questions in a gentle way or on another day.

Really dig deep into the lives of your family members. Use these questions to do it! As you ask the right questions, you'll find the gold within your family—the memories, moments, and stories that your family will hold onto for years to come.

ACTION ITEM: Assemble a simple list of questions and decide who you will interview. You may first want to ask a spouse, sibling, or child so that you can practice asking the questions, using any dictation equipment, and taking notes. This will let you become comfortable with the interview process. After this first interview, make your list of everyone you want to talk with and start interviewing your family. You will always treasure the stories you capture from each and every person in your family. They will be delighted when you give them a copy of their memories—they may remember more and want to be interviewed again!

8

REPURPOSE ACTIVITIES AND GAMES

*R*epurpose things you already have experience with. If you enjoyed something in one form, you may just enjoy it more using family history and stories. What did you enjoy doing as a child? What do your children enjoy doing? These are the kinds of things you will want to repurpose for family history.

My children loved playing with paper dolls when they were little. I was thinking about that and wondered if there was a family history activity that I could create with paper dolls.

I found a wonderful artist on Fiverr.com (lovepixels) that draws stylish cartoon characters from your photos. I had her draw my grandfather as a cartoon figure. My grandfather was a farmer, a mechanic, a soldier, and a good family man. So I asked her to duplicate my character four times, each wearing four different clothing styles. I also had her draw me the blackline masters of the same four dolls. This now gave me four coloring book pages and four color paper dolls.

I was hoping this would be a perfect activity for my little grandsons.

I printed out the color pictures and laminated the sheets. Now the children could cut out the paper grandpas, make a stand for them to stand upright, and then play away. I imagined them shooting them with rubber bands to knock them over or doing some imaginative active play. They play with super-hero action figures all the time. Why not a hero that truly lived? Maybe they'd put a farmer out in the grass and pretend he was farming. Maybe they'd gather all the toy animals and let the Grandpa Poe doll watch over his animals.

Some of my grandchildren did play with them! Others just built the stand up paper doll and put on the dressers or window sills as decorations.

On the coloring book pages, they could color each picture and read a short vignette about their great grandfather. For example, on the farmer coloring page, they can read: "Fowler Martin Poe was born on a farm on March 20, 1914 and grew up farming. He loved to farm. He quit school at fourteen years old to farm full-time. He grew cotton and corn and vegetables. He loved being a farmer."

I know. It's basic and repetitive. I meant it to be. I envisioned this for younger, early readers. When you ask one of the little boys if they know something about Grandpa Poe, they will respond, "He was a farmer." They have a simple story about a family member.

Along with the four coloring book pages and one laminated sheet of all four color dolls, I included a nineteen-page life story that included pictures and documents.

Fowler was a soldier in World War II. He went into the Army in 1942 and got out in 1945. He was an infantry man and was shot in the right elbow during the war. He earned a purple heart and two bronze stars.

The life history stayed on the same four themes that the paper dolls had. The life history had information about farming, several military pictures, his discharge papers from World War II, some family pictures, and his work information as a mechanic. I presented the simple knowledge for the children, then deepened and expanded upon the detailed life history for their parents Grandpa Poe's military discharge gave the adult men an interesting document to pick up and read to see his military history, combat medals awarded, battles and campaigns he fought in, as well as his length of service and separation pay. The women enjoyed a copy of the marriage record and pictures of the little love notes he left his wife. See? A little something for everyone. It piqued interest without a lengthy biography.

Now picture the moment. A package from Grandma arrives in the mail. What could it be? It opens up with a paper craft for the children and coloring book pages. It also has a history with pictures. While the children do the activity, the parent flips through the life story. Maybe they read a little. Maybe they just look at the pictures. The children ask questions, and the parents answer from the life history. The interaction and discussion could be bonding as both child and parent learn and talk together about a man that none of them knew. See the multigenerational interaction going on? We have a connection between Great-Grandpa Poe, Grandma (me), my children, my grandchildren. It's fun. It's family history.

And what was this like for me?

- First, I played with the genealogy, stories, pictures, and documents I had. That in itself, gave me fun for several days while I daydreamed about how to do it and assembled the booklet.
- Second, I passed on to my children and grandchildren activities and information that allowed them to share with each other and have story conversations about this ancestor.
- Third, I shared our family history in a fun and meaningful way to people not interested in genealogy.
- Fourth, I honored my grandfather's birthday by

introducing him to posterity he never met before his death.

As a big bonus, my Grandpa Poe's story has now been shared with more than a hundred family members through stories, pictures, documents, and—yes, you guessed it—paper dolls. See how you can repurpose something to make family history fun?

You can repurpose almost any game and make them into a family history game. If your family likes Old Maid, you can create a matching game with pictures of family members to match together. If they like hopscotch, instead of numbers in each square, you can place things related to your ancestors such as outlines of US states they lived in or copied pictures. If they like Scrabble, play a family history version where you can only make names and hometowns of relatives. If they enjoy pin the tail on the donkey, you can play pin the mustache on Dad or hand Mother an apple pie. If you play charades, you can play the family version, acting out events in your family, vacations you took, or things your family does together. You can play Pictionary the same way. Playing Family Story Bingo lets you play with your family while you are sharing family stories or pictures. They won't even know!

You can search the internet for more ideas for your family history games. With these games, the whole family will have a new type of fun that brings intergenerational closeness. Let's play with our family history. As we find ways to repurpose what we already know and love, we can come to know and love our ancestors even more.

ACTION ITEM: Watch your family doing things they consider fun. Think about how you can take the activity and repurpose it. Make it into a family history game or give it a family history theme.

9

A FAMILY DIGEST

*D*o you enjoy the magazine "Reader's Digest"? When I buy a copy, I read it cover to cover and then offer it to my eleven-year-old grandson. He loves to read and will read anything. He enjoys the variety; it is perfect for his attention span and now he has his own subscription. Let "Reader's Digest" be your structure for your impossible goal of creating a family story. Write like that!

On the Reader's Digest website you can see what the magazine strives to do:

"Reader's Digest unites its readers and their families like no other brand through the simplest of acts: sharing stories, laughs, and great advice. . . . [The magazine stands out] due to its themes of optimism, faith, heroism, trust, humor, and wellness. . . . [Online articles give readers] peace of mind, and save them time and money, by helping them know exactly what and what not to worry about. . . . [Their books] deliver a bundle of emotions from curiosity and amazement to reassurance, gratitude, and amusement. In all its work, Reader's Digest carries on its singular, historic vision: to bring out the good in people and families everywhere" (www.rd.com/about-readers-digest/).

We can take on a similar mission to bring out the good in our families. And the best part is that you don't have to be a genealogist or family historian to take this as your mission. You just need to want to belong and have others belong and connect with you.

This magazine has found not only a great purpose, but also a great format—both of which you can incorporate into your own family storytelling. Notice how there is variety in each edition. There is a serious story, an inspirational story, an informational story, followed by quotes or jokes or pictures. All stories have different lengths and different topics. I like how I feel when I read a "Reader's Digest," and I like the things I learn.

We can use this pattern.

Start your collection of family stories by thinking of it as "[Your Last Name] Digest." For me, it's the "Gormley Digest." What will your collection be called? Next, write an introductory page that tells your relatives why you are creating this family digest. This is a mission statement or an "Editor's Note" of sorts.

The next step is to mix in any stories you have. Some long, some short. Some funny, some sad. Include some one-liners and some geographical references. Mix up any family history content any way you want. You can put in one ancestor picture and one contemporary picture. You can take a picture of a family object and explain what it is, where it came from, who has it, and why it's a family treasure. Add any picture or whatever you have.

Put some content in the Family Digest that will get your readers—your family members—involved. Have a questions page that asks your relatives to write in with their answers or memories. You could enlist "guest writers" to share something. Anything. They can tell about themselves, a pet, a memory, or something current going on in their lives. You can make a call for artwork from the little ones in your family, shrink it down, and print a "Today's Children" page. Then the children will be interested to have their own copy! Call on parents to tell a short story on one of their children's latest jokes, questions, comments, or perspectives. Invite family members to look through their social media posts and pick one to be inserted in your Family Digest. Announce a contest and encourage people to write in with something. For example, you could include a picture of a family vacation or activity long ago, and then ask all the children to contribute their memories of that vacation or activity for the next Digest. Those that contribute, get a prize. Or those that don't, get a loser prize.

If you are worried that some relative may overshare, limit each story submission to one paragraph or one hundred words or less. As you talk and interact with family, take notes and write like a newspaper gossip columnist would: "It seems firemen were called to the Rice home with a chimney fire on Christmas day . . ."

Now, starting your own family magazine may seem overwhelming. But this project can be fun, affordable, and simple. If you start building on it a little at a time, this Family Digest can stay easy and grow throughout the years. Your editor's note can say the digest will appear randomly whenever you get enough contributions from others. Eventually, you may be able to send out something regularly. Your own Family Digest can become a most anticipated publication each month or each quarter.

You can keep this project free by saving it in Word or PDF and simply emailing it out to family members. If you have a family Facebook group, you can upload it to the group and let them get it themselves. It all stays easy and free. After you have sent out monthly magazines for a year, you can send out an end-of-the-year or a first-of-the-year volume with content from all twelve months.

What makes sense for you and your family dynamics?

How about a "Family Digest Just for Kids"? If you are a grandparent and want to emphasize your history and storytelling to your grandchildren, perhaps dedicate a third of the magazine's pages to the stories or facts on ancestors, a third about you (history or current activities), and a third on the grandchildren. This way, your focus is clear, and your grandchildren get to know their ancestors, you, and their cousins.

Ask your grandchildren to send you pictures of themselves, school projects or activities, or jokes. Then, compile them and send them out to every grandchild. The first page can be about you and the rest of the pages can be about them. It becomes a simple family summary of sorts that in the years to come may be a treasure capturing their childhood. You can email it out monthly and snail mail out the one year collection each Christmas as part of your Christmas card or Christmas present. Lots of people send out Christmas newsletters, but you and your grandchildren will enjoy a unique multi-generational year in review. If money is an issue, ask your children for contributions to print and give out the year's Family Digest each Christmas. Their investment into your "hobby" is an investment in their own children's family love, connections, memories, and resilience.

What do you want your Family Digest to be?

Let's go back to the "Reader's Digest" quote: Their magazine has "themes of optimism, faith, heroism, trust, humor, and wellness." Isn't that what we want for our families? When speaking to our child, we may tend to sound negative and say things like, "Julie, if you would only listen to me . . ." But when we write in our Family Digest, we can give advice that's softer and much more positive: "One of the best pieces of advice I ever had was from my grandmother. She cautioned me to . . . and it worked for me!" What a wonderful and easy way for a parent or grandparent to give advice and wisdom! If we make it generic, it is less likely to offend.

We can write out what we think is optimistic and then have time to self-check and edit so it really is optimistic and hope-promoting, rather than a negative. The value of taking the time in writing and then editing allows us to filter our words, stories, and advice and provide welcomed life lessons without harshness or judgment. Reality is that some things or people are negative and some family members may disappoint us, but the trick is to digest those things and then provide bright and beautiful reflections of and for our families. I learned long ago to treat people as I wanted them to be. It isn't easy, but I have found that, if I treat others *as if* they measured up to my expectations, that 1) I was happier, and 2) I didn't show my disapproval.

Again, the "Reader's Digest" publications strive to "deliver a bundle of emotions from curiosity and amazement to reassurance, gratitude, and amusement." Is not this our goal of sharing more of our family's story with our families? Don't we want them to be curious about each member of our family and our history? Don't we want them to be amazed at our lives and their own potential? Don't we want to reassure them that just as our ancestors worked through the past, they can too? Don't we want them to be grateful for their family, past and present? Don't we want them to laugh and have amusement at our own missteps?

Yes, the "Reader's Digest" is an excellent pattern for those who want to build on the central theme of bringing out the best of our families.

ACTION ITEM: Try the "Reader's Digest" format out for yourself. Write for a positive and educational purpose. Write for fun and insight. Write jokes, share pictures, and include quotes. Pick some themes and see if you can find your own experiences that illustrate those themes. Keep each section brief. Don't overcomplicate your efforts. Let others participate, and see if you can get out your family's digest as a Christmas or New Year's present for the whole family.

10

QUITE THE CHARACTER

"*I* can't write stories."

"I just don't know what to write."

If writing is what's getting in the way of you capturing your life story or your family's stories, let's try another way of thinking about it. Think of your favorite television show, movie, or book. How easy is it to tell someone about it? You know every character and what makes them tick. You know the story line. Some things are disappointing, and some things are so exciting that you can't wait to talk with someone about it! You'll find that telling someone the story from a tv show isn't all that different from telling the story of someone's life. And talking about fictional characters isn't too different from talking about your family. Using this tv show comparison, you can practice and improve your ability to write stories.

Let's do this exercise together. Start with any fictional character you intensely love, and describe the character in detail. Give examples of moments that show us who the character is and why. Write down the general premise of the show. Next, read online reviews and summaries to see what you could have added that you missed. Also notice if you totally agree with others or if you disagree with others. This will give you perspective and help you realize how subjective storytelling can be.

With your show summarized and the characters sketched out, write what you think the purpose of the show is or what the entertainment value is. Can you provide the show's values? Do you know what is important to each character?

Now that you have done a favorite show, try pretending you are the main character. After all, you are the star in your own life story! You have a storyline as well as supporting characters. You have experiences, hopes, dreams, motivations, and values—just like a character on a show. The same way you talk about a character and their world, you can talk about yourself and your life.

Use this way of thinking when learning how or what to write in your family history stories. Try writing about yourself, ancestors, and living family members in the "tv way." If we were going to write you as a character and write out everyone you know as a character, how would we do it? First, we could draft a character sketch. Below is a template that you can use as you pull together your sketch. After you've created a character sketch for yourself, try doing one for a living family member or an ancestor you've never met.

Character Sketch

Physical Description:

You don't have to describe every single physical trait, but include the important things. Some ideas are hair type, hair color, eye color, body type, height, and skin tone. You could include distinguishing features like tattoos, clothing styles, voice, posture, scent, gestures, or mannerisms.

Best Traits:

Think of what traits best describe you. What values do you show? Are you friendly, confident, and humorous? Are you loyal, disciplined, and organized? Here are some more ideas for words you could use: bold, courageous, cautious, kind, respectful, responsible, reliable, trustworthy, honest, humble, fair, empathetic, compassionate, generous, polite, happy, loving, people-oriented, goal-oriented, hard worker, open, curious, charming, patient, clear headed, smart, street-smart, intelligent, studious, well-read, wise, leader, and follower. (I could go on forever.)

Less Flattering Traits:

Maybe only pick one or two. Don't spend too much time on this one, and don't hurt your feelings or others' feelings. Some ideas can include laziness, pride, greed, stubbornness, unkindness. You can also pick a trait that you used to have but have worked on.

Background Story:

In a good book, tv show, or movie, you usually don't see a character's backstory, but it is hinted at in some way. You know something of the person without it having been shown to you explicitly. For example, part of the backstory might be that the character had good or bad parents. They have had a good or poor education. Were they religious or non-religious growing up? These backstory experiences affect their today.

There are many times we want to share why we are the way we are. We all have pivotal moments in our lives. On a television show, we discover them and suddenly understand a character's motivations or actions. Look at yourself as a character. What is your backstory? What is a past event or experience that changed you in a profound way? As you are writing out your short backstory, ask yourself what the interesting historical parts are of your life that have made you who you are today. Do you want to reveal those?

Five Things About the Character that Need Fixing:

I could have labeled this as a weakness, but I want you to think of this one as if you could change. In your television show, every character has something that needs to be fixed. You want them to fix it, or you can clearly see how this thing often trips them up. This can be applied to your own character sketch. How would you change yourself? How would you change a family member? Maybe you would give them confidence, more education, the ability to not be hurtful or take offense, or the ability to be quicker to ask or open up. Sketching out yourself as if you're a fictitious character allows you to focus on sketching out your personality as others may see you in their lives. From this exercise, you may see that you have parts of you that need fixing in your story and you can set about now to strengthen your weaknesses or make right past mistakes. This is a lovely start to creating for yourself a better life story.

Quirks:

There are hundreds of quirks you can include in your character sketch. Here are just a few: braggy, enthusiastic, attention-seeking, obsessive about something, always late, always early, Pollyanna type, overly sensitive, speaks to loud, speaks too soft, jokester.

You could also include any physical quirks like the following: bites lips, bites fingernails, jingles keys, plays with hair, hums, intense or no eye contact, sniffs or coughs a lot, giggles, uses their hands to talk, snorts when laughing, slurps, speaks to loudly or too softly, eats too fast or too slow, snacks too much or never, shuffles feet, bouncy walking, scratches head or pulls ears, limps, has unique posture, articulate, dresses in only one style, doesn't seem to care how they are dressed, always has a possession on them (sunglasses, backpack, watch, or toothpick).

Annoying or Endearing Habits:

This is a weird one because what annoys one person another finds quite endearing and vice versa. These would include any strengths, weaknesses, or quirks that you've already written down. Picking up on your own annoying habits can be a challenge, but try. If you want to be brave, ask someone you trust to give you only one of your habits. (You want to keep a good relationship!) Maybe you talk while chewing, slurp drinks, snore, use way too much perfume or cologne, tap your feet, drum with your fingers on everything, don't put lids on things, click pens, or put socks on the floor instead of in the laundry basket.

I once determined I wanted to be kinder. After actively working on showing kindness each day for a time, no one even noticed. Sometimes our annoying habits are clearly known and other times not so much.

Strengths:

Refer to the "Best Traits" section above. But also think about what you would say about yourself in a job interview. These might be personality strengths or skill strengths. It is often hard to think of our strengths, but think of it this way: What would others say your strengths are? Are you a leader, follower, hard worker, or quick thinker? Are you detail-oriented or are you a big picture thinker?

What are you good at? Put anything you're good at or love doing in this category of strengths. Maybe you're good at math, caring for children, typing, photography, driving, fixing computers, money management, teaching, building, repairs, auto mechanics, reading, communicating, cooking, baking, enduring, adapting, mental strength, physical strength, or emotional strength.

What the Character Learned:

Can you identify lessons you have learned? If not, what lessons would you like to learn? How have you grown or changed over time? Think about it in different ways and decide how you want others to see your growth.

How do you learn? Perhaps you learn through experiencing things, fixing a mistake or error, reading, watching, talking with others, or taking classes.

How can you learn? Maybe you can improve how you learn through goal setting, practice, effort, or asking for help.

We do not typically evaluate our growth or learning. Often, it is a parent that can identify the learned lessons for a child. Parents can help children realize that an experience is teaching them something or that they take away something specific from the experience. Put yourself in that parental mindset when you do this activity for yourself. Write the experience and then ponder what you did learn and what you could have learned. Were you the same and didn't let it affect you, or were you different afterwards? We learn resiliency through practical application of our experiences.

I hope at this point you have several pages about yourself. Now go back and ask yourself *how* you know these things about yourself and tell a story about each one. Give an example experience. Write them as paragraphs.

"I think I am loyal because . . ."

"Others said I was good at time management because I helped . . ."

As you write actual experiences, you are building your own story. You're proving or finding your character traits and experiences, giving value and meaning to them. This is an excellent way to tell your best personal history. It's also a good start to recognizing and developing traits you want but are not evident or strong in your life story so far. You may feel you are loving but don't show it. Now you can make the change to show it.

I wanted you to do your favorite television show and fictional character first, because it seems less daunting and less personal. You can easily talk about the television show with its characters, because it is safe to sketch out something fictitious. If you were able to do your favorite show, you can do your own life using the same process.

By setting down and completing your own character sketch, you will write your life story with more direction, meaning, and purpose. If you can articulate your attributes and draw upon your experiences, you can follow the character sketch using the paragraph format.

"I think I am strong in this. These are two or three examples that show this."

"I am this way, and this is why. Or this is how I learned to be this way."

It doesn't have to read like a narrative from birth to death. You can write yourself in this attribute format and give examples with experience.

You are reliving or retelling the stories that make you *you*. You are finding the things you want to share with your current family or your future posterity. Anything you don't want to tell, you skip! Use those things as inspiration to make the changes you need to make. The purpose of this book is to help you write your treasured personal and family history, so write about yourself at your best.

Take the time to think it through and add to it. If you can't go from the character sketch to the experience, then do it backwards and discover a character trait you didn't know you had. Tell the story then find what it reveals about you. Remember this is all subjective to find the experience, identify your feelings, what you learned and how it might help others. After you write it, it may be raw, so let it sit. You can go back a few days later and soften word choices or find the bigger meaning.

I want you to write your personal history as your best self. Share the stories that bring others joy and understanding concerning you and other family members. Write the stories that will strengthen and encourage anyone that reads it. Our posterity may learn resiliency and wisdom by applying what they learn from our lives. We can help them overcome, because we once or many-times-over overcame. We can help them keep a good perspective because we've done the same thing. They can go into the tunnel because they saw us come out the other side. They can face setbacks, disappointments, fears, and tragedies because we did. Your history might provide your descendants with the vision and the confidence to keep going.

Don't forget the purpose of writing your stories. We write our stories so that we can strengthen and deepen our relationships with our family. These character sketches help get us there.

ACTION ITEMS:

- Create a character sketch of your favorite television character. Then, give examples from the show that reveal the character's traits.
- Create a character sketch of yourself. Then, give examples in your life that reveal your traits.

11

TRADES AND OCCUPATIONS

*M*y father earned a degree in accounting and had many positions over the years. Some were very prestigious. But no matter what the position he held, if you asked him what he did, he always replied, "I am an accountant." Because we preserved his last résumé, we have an excellent understanding of what he did in his long career. The next part we are missing is what *he* thought about it. What were his thoughts, feelings, motivations? What were his best stories about being an accountant?

It was at my father's funeral that many coworkers at every level shared their memories of what kind of person my father was at work. They described him as helpful, willing, friendly, kind, and honest - among other traits -and they gave us example memories. What a treasure that became to have insights into the man at work. How glad I am that we wrote them down and have more color on his work life. My father's occupation and the interaction he had with people at his work helped us to understand more about him.

If I tell you my story or someone else's story, it's easy to make the mistake of giving an occupation but then too quickly moving on to other things. Let's take more time writing about the trade or occupation part of our lives. If you are telling your own story, spend extra time on your life's work. Share why you went into that field of study or trade. Did you have a mentor? Did you find the work itself rewarding or did you do it for the salary? Do you have work experiences you can share? What exactly did you do?

Let me share an example of how I collected information about one of my family member's occupations and how I shared it with others. My great-grandfather, William Gormley, was a saddler and had his own shop for decades in the downtown square of Huntsville, Alabama. While researching his life and sharing it out, I could easily just stop there and move on to other historical facts. Instead, I used this little snippet of information and searched the internet for "saddler" and discovered what a saddler did. Then, a quick search on YouTube allowed me to find and watch someone work as a saddler. I searched on newspapers.com to find a copy of old Huntsville, Alabama newspapers, and I actually found one of my great-grandfather's advertisements in the paper.

The Democrat (Huntsville, Alabama)
21 Jun 1832, Thu page 1

Now I can more fully share that he was saddler with a description of what he did. I can find a coloring book page to share with little children and have family members watch the YouTube video with me. I can also show his advertisement in the paper. Taking additional steps can help us relate to our family members, expand our personal knowledge of different occupations, and appreciate our family members' work in a new way.

You can share information either through a story you tell or as a conversation starter. Let's say I'm in the car and see a horse in the field. I can say, "You know, your grandfather William Gormley was a saddler and would have made the saddle to put on that horse." Talk about an opening remark that could take off into conversation! Or it could just be an offhand comment that has everyone in the car nodding and the subject changes. But now they know! The more that you know about your family's lives, including their work life, the more you are able to share.

Rather than learn about only one of your family member's occupations, you can make it a new project of yours to learn all the jobs in the family. Make a list of occupations for your whole family. By sharing the occupations of each family member and a little something about their jobs, you help your relatives connect with their ancestors. Now you are writing a history of occupations in your extended family. It's easy to write about everyone at once because the only subject you're homing in on is occupation.

Compiling a collection of all known occupations in your family now and over time can be interesting all by itself. Do you have a great variety of family occupations? Or do you have several generations of farmers, teachers, musicians, lawyers, or factory workers?

I know you want to do your four generations of ancestors and even share one of those stellar ancestors that was an outlaw or a founding father. And you certainly can do just that. But don't forget to share the occupations of living family members too. It might be the best place to start! Think of it as chapter one for the living and chapter two for the past.

How can you go about collecting the family occupations? Start by listing out everyone in your family. Write down the education and occupation of every family member. Then, send out a text or email to each person and tell them you are making a family résumé. Ask them if they would please send back to you a paragraph of what they do. If you could get everyone to give you a few lines, you will have documented your current family as of the year you do it.

I can hear some of you saying, "What about people that don't have an occupation?" Simple! Don't think of occupation exclusively as a career or job. An occupation can be how one stays occupied—how they occupy their time. It is a snapshot photo taken today of their life's work. If they are a student, they can share why they are going to school and what they hope to become. If they are a homemaker, unemployed, retired, or at home for whatever other reason, they can share what they did previously and how they spend their time now.

Tell everyone that you want to make a little booklet and capture your family's story of occupations as of today and that you will be sharing it with everyone. If you have people like my dad in your family, don't be satisfied with "I am an accountant." Also, if you ask someone what they do and they tell you raising children, ask all the same questions that you might apply to a workforce job. Each life's work is interesting and valuable. You may want to send a list of questions they can respond to for uniformity. Here are some questions you could ask:

1. What is your current occupation/life's work?
2. How did you learn this trade or what school did you go to?
3. What is your favorite thing about this work?
4. What is your best or favorite moment in your working life?
5. How long have you done this job?
6. Why do you do your job (besides money)? What do you enjoy about it?
7. What advice would you give to someone starting this job?

Having ten brothers and sisters, I might struggle writing a short bio on each person. But if I request little bits of information each month (like occupation) over a year or so, I could compile a simple, straightforward summary of everyone. And it would be from them! You can do this for more than just occupations too—you can also collect lists of hobbies, places they have lived, vacations, schools, religions, values, memories of another family member, and so on. I could never get a sibling to sit and write their history for me answering fifty questions, but if I email them a little survey or questionnaire each month, I could have a solid summary at the end of the year. It would be better than nothing. Or it can be a great building block for further writing, telling, and sharing their story.

A list of occupations can serve all the family, but it can especially help teenagers and young adults. When young family members look at the list of all their aunts', uncles', and cousins' occupations, they may want to ask questions, build a rapport with someone, or go back to school. They didn't know their uncle was so cool, or they knew their aunt was cool but now they know why! See? You just piqued their interest in their own family. Knowing what relatives do for a living can help youth have the courage to ask their uncle how he chose his career or how they could get that kind of education. They may be more likely to ask for help in writing a résumé or applying for positions. The extended family can be mentors for the progress of our children. I have directed my own children to call an uncle for insight or guidance on higher education or professional careers. Many of us have helped polish résumés and helped prep for interviews. Here is one great area wherein the strength of a unified family can be of great benefit to the rising generation.

If you are writing your own story, ponder more deeply about recording your occupation or life's work. What would you imagine others would share about you around the water cooler or at your retirement party or at your funeral? You can share some of those stories, insights, and attributes now. Write down your best and worst days at work. Write your daily routine so that others can see a sample of what your days looked like. What were your biggest successes, regrets, strengths, and weaknesses? It is easy to write topically and group it together in a chapter or booklet. After a few weeks of a different topic every week or month, you will soon have a wonderful personal story. Let a trusted family member or friend read it, and then ask them if they had any questions while reading it. Was anything not answered or left out that they wanted to know? What could you add to it?

You can write a work story with the intent to inspire, share a lesson learned, or just give your family a laugh. I have a funny story that happened to me while I was interviewing for a promotion within my company. Although it's not about my work, it happened at work! And it sure is a funny story—one that my family still smiles about when it is mentioned. That is the story I want them to tell with delight a hundred years from now. That is the story worthy of a comedy sketch on any television show. It is the only funny story I can think about after more than a decade of working at that company. One funny story in fifteen years? Yes, just one, but it's a great one. I hope your curiosity is stirred and you are wanting me to tell it. See? That is the power of a story. If it is not shared, it is lost.

ACTION ITEM: How many family occupations do you already know? Write a list of all your living family members and a second, separate list of all the deceased family members you know. Can you write beside each of their names their work or trade? Do you have any physical item from their work? Do you know why they chose that occupation? Sharing more of your family's story can be about discovering and sharing more about what their work life was like.

12

BE THE STORY GATHERER

*T*ell your children's stories *to* your children. My bedtime stories were typically stories about the child I was talking to. I would retell a fairy tale, inserting my child's name as the character and allow them to be the hero of the story. I'd be so proud that Little Sally Riding Hood had outsmarted the wolf and saved the grandmother, and I'd give them the moral of the story or the life lesson they could take from it.

Instead of a fairy tale retelling, I would sometimes retell an actual event from that child's day. I'd reframe it to be a positive or proud moment for that child. The last interaction the child had before falling asleep was the thought that he had shown bravery, courage, intelligence, compassion, or whatever the story conveyed. Use these stories to remind little children of their accomplishments, positive traits, and ways you are proud of them. Your children will love it when you fashion a bedtime story about them and tell a true story with a life's lesson.

Are your children all grown up, far away for school or work, or have families of their own now? You can still sit down and write a simple story about them. Write something you remember fondly or appreciate in their character. It doesn't have to be long. You can write it on a postcard—a 5X7 index card. Put an inexpensive postcard-rate stamp on it and send it. You can write it out or type it out on a piece of paper and mail it in an envelope for the cost of a stamp. You can send a text that says, "I was remembering how fun it was when you made that touchdown in middle school. I was cheering you on. I hope you made a touchdown today at work. Love, Mother."

The occasional text, short email, or postcard does at *least* two things: 1) It strengthens the current relationship by sharing a happy memory you both share, and 2) it preserves and connects each of you to a historical moment to be remembered. Often, I think it also improves the day for each person. It's an expression of love, joy, and happiness that affirms you think of each other in loving and respectful ways. It's a long-distance hug or kiss.

When I send birthday cards or emails to my children, I often will rehearse to them the day of their birth including things like the weather, time of day, who was there, how special it was to meet them, why they were named, what they were, and so on. Any and every memory is offered for that day. It gives them their own history, and it reminds them I love them.

I like to send or share occasional reminders to a child about their favorite toy, pet, tv show, things to do, and food to eat. It is easy to find a picture of old toys on the internet and share it out. "Guess what I found? A picture of your favorite doll when you were five." You can also send notes that show appreciation for your family member such as: "I appreciated that you always mowed the lawn for me" (or did the dishes or helped with other children).

I view this way of reaching out to children the same way I view Facebook's "On This Day" feature. Facebook shows you memories from that particular day a year, two years, or ten years ago. This bit of history can be reshared on your page or just bring a bit of happiness to you for that immediate moment. Now, is there such a thing as getting too many of these? Maybe. You may not want to be reminded of the past and your old self (or others) constantly.

When sharing these memories and stories with your children, be wise in how frequently you send them. Just as Facebook allows you to block the "On This Day" notifications, your family might want to block you. You don't want them to groan when they see an email, text, card, or letter from you. Use sparingly if you don't know how they are received. Use generously if they are welcomed.

Another caution: We often ruin a memory by attaching some remark or a "wish you would call more" lecture. Always be positive and never include any type of barb. For example, I have an adult son that has the same car I bought him when he was sixteen. It was an old cash car even then. Now, fourteen years later, he is still driving that car. We can tease him about driving a piece of junk around, or we can admire his ability to save money, live within his means, and not go into debt. Even though he may no longer need to be frugal after college graduation, he has a good financial habit of value and thrift. It is all about how you frame something.

Every family has a little bit of everything; we all have strengths and failings. Let's craft our personal and family stories to strengthen and build people. I would rather share a family story that builds and encourages rather than mocks or derides. Do your stories teach your children to praise or to mock others? Do they instill confidence or insecurity? Do they share joy or misery? Family stories are a great way for you to measure the perspectives or attitudes you are passing on to your children and grandchildren.

If you have a family story that is negative, write it down and really look at it. Ponder it. If you can reframe it positively for the person, rewrite it with that mindset and review it again. Does it come off as positive now? Let a trusted friend read the story and see if it does. If not, rewrite it again or discard. There is no reason to pass along a fresh reminder that someone failed. Perhaps send a different kind of note, make the phone call, or knock on the door and say the words, "I am so sorry I hurt you when . . ." Use a negative story from the past to heal and repair relationships. This turns a negative story from yesterday into a positive story today.

Gathering up your living family's stories can be a fun and rewarding activity for you. It's an easy, low-cost hobby to fill the hours of retirement, sleepless nights, or the wait time before an appointment or during an oil change. All you need is pen and paper or a computer to type. You can write them as vignettes, a brief account of an event or characteristic. You can make a folder for each person, and as you think of any memory, you write it down and put it in their folder. Just collect them for years if you want to. When they come to visit, they can look through their folder and have wonderful little stories of their lives as seen through your eyes. At the end of every year or at every birthday, you can assemble them and send as a personal present. It is nice to hear good things about yourself or remember things forgotten in the daily present.

This is what I love about living history. You don't have to think of it as a project. It is just a daily or weekly activity of putting pen to paper and recording memories of loved ones. For you, it can be an activity that brings you joy and strengthens your mind. For them, it can be a gift that brings them confidence and reminds them of happy times. For posterity, it can be perhaps the only way to find out what their parents were like as children. In today's social communication we call this connection, but I still describe this as enduring bonds of love and family.

Imagine if today, someone gave you a folder of stories of your great-grandparent's birth, childhood, adulthood, thoughts, and feelings. What a treasure it would be to know someone you do not know. That will be a gift you can give in the future. Your posterity will someday have a treasure of your accounts of the people you loved.

Allow your hands to be the loving hands that record your family's stories. As they read them, not only will the story you tell be made known to them, but your love will be between the lines.

ACTION ITEM:

- Look for opportunities to tell your children's stories to them. You can tell them a simple memory as you visit with them, or through text, phone call, or email.
- Write and collect stories of a family member in a folder. During a special occasion, gift your collection to the person.

13

THE POWER OF PERSPECTIVE

*a*re you in the middle of your *own* story? Guess what? We all are. Even though you are in the middle of living your story, the exercise of writing it can have a positive impact for you—it can sharpen your focus and help you determine next steps in your life. As you develop the writer's perspective, you'll see that your past self is ready and prepared to meet today's moment, and you'll look forward to being your future self.

You can use writing and sharing your own story to see where you come from and what path you are on. Writing your story gives you the opportunity to look back at your life. Record the events and decisions you've made that have brought you to this moment. You may be able to see that your choices brought you here, and you can give yourself some advice for how to do things differently moving forward. Or maybe you'll see that where you are now has little to do with your decisions and more to do with an interruption that happened. Maybe you're at a particularly good moment in your life; write the things that brought you to this good moment. Share what you hope to accomplish. Share your plans to successfully navigate the days ahead. You can have peace, even during difficulties, because of the perspective you choose to take in each of life's moments.

One thing you learn as a historian is that the past is perspective. Yes, the historian may have hundreds or thousands of primary or secondary sources, but they choose from those sources a narrative they want to convey. The historian is not objective. They are framing or reframing a perspective from their sources.

News can be the same way. Different news organizations tell the same story in different ways or spin it differently. It's all perspective. Look at the word choices people use to describe something. They influence your perspective by choosing inflammatory words or positive words. They use not only words, but facial expressions and gestures to influence you to feel sympathy or sadness. They may influence you to take some action due to their presentation.

As a personal historian, we often hear the same story told by several different people. They each have a different perspective. These varying perspectives could be due to age or the impact the event had on them. They could tell the story differently to protect themselves or someone else in the story. Now, I'm not suggesting that you manipulate, twist, or omit the truth. Without advising you to make your stories up,

I am asking you to consider an event from several perspectives.

Watch your own word choices. Read it out loud, and see how it sounds. Does the event still bring you the same emotion it did at the time? Did you learn anything from it? Move past it? Can you relate the event and then say, "That event was for me to learn from" or "That event taught me" or even "I can forgive myself or him/her because I am no longer that person"?

I learned that every day could be a bad day or a good day depending on my mood and what I place emphasis on. Every day typically has good, bad, and boring in it. What is your perspective? If you are in a difficult or lonely place right now, list all the events that you think have brought you to this moment. Then try reframing them to find positive value. If you are in a good place right now, list all the events that brought you to this moment. Tell those stories through various lenses and perspectives.

While writing our own life stories, we can take the time to ponder the meaning we are assigning to the past and discover if we've learned anything from the event. I can tell you that I and my ten siblings all experienced the same family events. Some thought an event was a big deal, others thought it was nothing. Others didn't even remember the event. It is all a matter of age and perspective—and the meaning we each assigned it. We can decide if we see the glass half full, half empty, or just a glass with something neither good nor bad in it. We shouldn't let unhelpful or hurtful thoughts influence our lives.

Part of this personal history exercise is just for you. Take the time to write or ponder events and important moments in your life. What did it mean to you and why did you give it that meaning? Can you see different meanings or values? Are you limiting your perspective? Are you overvaluing (sugar coating) things or undervaluing (dismissing) things?

This is actually a good way to play with your own history. Write an event from different points of view. Write the event as a positive and a negative. What feels natural and comfortable? Write the memory from a matter-of-fact-only point of view. Which version would you want others to keep 100 or 500 years from now?

I think family history has helped me personally become my best self. I learned from my ancestors' stories and documents. I wondered why things happened to people in the family like they did. I wonder if I had the whole picture. Was my ancestor actually sad or depressed, or were they just tired and had health issues? Did my ancestor's parents divorce due to marital issues, or did they not process a tragedy together? Did ancestors that came to America miss their home country, or was it the land of promise they hoped it would be?

Writing and analyzing my own stories helps broaden my perspective as well. I wonder why I chose that word. I wonder if that event was a pivotal moment that changed me, or was that always who I was and it just needed to be revealed? I ask myself, "How did this experience serve me?"

Then, I determine I either need to let go of it (it is a negative experience that doesn't serve me) or embrace it (it made me better, stronger, and happier).

In this way, playing with our personal history allows us to self-coach. We can search for positives, benefits, life lessons and build a more positive future for ourselves. We can notice that when we write a story, we use negative words or phrases. And if we just change the word, the meaning is better and clearer. I remember once a woman said that she was an ornery teenager. She meant the word as argumentative or debating. Someone reflected back to her that she had said she was a bad teenager, but that wasn't the intent at all. One person said she was discouraged, and another took it for depressed. Those may be two very different things.

When I write my thoughts out, I also wonder if this was found decades later, would it do any good for others? Or if I record something true but horrible about an ancestor, would it do any good for others to know this long-lost fact? Who else and what else does a shared story affect? How can I turn this story into something that promotes faith or gives a lesson learned?

If you think, "I am going to play with my life story," you can start small by writing your story for the last month or capturing a recent event. Then, set it aside for a while and come back to it. Looking only at the word choices, are you positive or negative? Do you write generally, or do you get specific? Did you record factually or to make you or others look good or bad? Did you record facts or feelings? Did you learn anything from it?

You can use family history or, more specifically, your personal history to focus on effective ways to write with better meaning and more positive understanding. After you do this gentle life coaching, you can pull out another piece of paper and write your personal history with a better perspective and purpose.

Play with your own story before you write it for posterity. Taking some time to play with your perspective can give you a better understanding of the past as well as a brighter future.

Write your own story like you are writing a eulogy. What do you hope people will think of you and feel about you? Pretend you are standing to present at your own funeral your life story. What would you want shared? The important things, the funny things, and the things you were most proud of or pleased of. You want the audience to laugh with you, cry with you, and walk out of there loving you.

Sometimes an event or experience changes you forever. You can never be the same after it. You know it was a pivotal moment. Some people say they keep time before and after something happened to them: before or after marriage, before or after a birth of a child, before or after the death of a loved one, before or after an injury, hurt, new job, move, and so on. It can be a good experience or a hard one, but you know you are forever changed. Writing your personal history can be a moment like that for you.

If you are not the person you need to be, change. If your personal history doesn't read like you want, accept it as Scrooge accepted the message from the Ghost of Christmas Yet to Come, and change. Commit to better values or more positive time with family and friends. Commit to be better and more in whatever you want to be.

Writing your personal history allows you to see who you were in the past and allows you to create the path to become someone even better.

ACTION ITEM: Review all the perspectives you could have while gathering and sharing your story and your loved ones' stories. Be kind and positive in your perspective. Capture the best of yourself and your family. Give your remembrances some meaning, and frame them to help the next generation. Write the kind of history that will light the way for your loved ones that will follow you.

14

PICTURES AND STORIES

*a*ny day of boredom or sadness can be repurposed into a family history day. Sadness turns into joy by the end of the day if you've put a postcard in the mail to a loved one. You will find joy at the end of the day if you have sorted pictures, found old love letters to share, or called a family member. Family history brings joy.

Discovering a family member's past can change your today and your tomorrow. Just as an ancestor's past can change you, sharing *your* past with a family member can change *them*! Your own stories can strengthen and encourage your family and maybe generations more. Your own stories can attract your family to you. They will learn, laugh, love you, and want to interact with you. Shared knowledge and shared stories build relationships for a long-lasting family.

Complete this statement for different family members: "Knowing [something] about [a family member], helped me to be/learn/appreciate . . ." Can you complete the statement again and again, making a small list for all your family members—both living and deceased?

Hours or days of boredom can become your greatest blessing as you sit down with pen and paper and think. Write down thoughts and feelings. Recount past events. Find pictures and group them by timeframes or people. Take each picture, and describe the picture and the people in it. Write what you remember about the day the picture was taken, or write all the things that come into your mind regarding the picture. Later you can have someone copy your picture and attach the paper copy to the memories you record.

If you have an older family member, copy your pictures down on paper, no matter if the picture was taken last month or fifty years ago. Visit your relative and ask if they would write what they remember about the picture and the people in it. You will give them hours of pleasure to disrupt their boredom. Their boredom fades away and their heart is gladdened as their memories are remembered. They will enjoy the day, and you will have a treasure forever.

This concept of describing pictures is elementary. In first grade, teachers would give us a sheet of picture and story paper. We would draw a picture on the top of the page and then write a little description or story. It is so basic and so very easy.

Pictures and stories just go together so naturally, and there are many ways to put a picture in someone's hands and then listen to what they remember about it. The secret is to start thinking outside the box. How do we accomplish this? Do we go in person and do the activity with them? Do we send pictures via slow mail? Do we send them via email, text, or a social media platform? Tailor the *how* by the distance and technological abilities of the people you are interacting with. The *how* doesn't matter. It only matters that you achieve the outcome.

To do this activity across long distances, you can send ten copied pictures to a relative. Tell them you need their help identifying the pictures or getting more story, and let them know you will call them in a few days. They get a few days to enjoy the pictures, think on them, and look forward to your phone call. When you call, it may be a good idea to record it so that you don't miss anything they say. Alternatively, you can put them on speaker phone and have your children write down the story while you do the talking. You're having a valuable interaction between living family members and creating a lasting history together.

You can email or text a picture and then call the person and ask, "Can you tell me anything about this picture?" "How old are you in this picture?" "Where were you and who were you with?" Asking for the basics may just jog their memories. If you're lucky, they may just start pouring out a story to you! Capture the story, the thoughts, and the feelings. Express your love for them, and thank them for their precious time and attention.

Boredom in children can be handled the same way. Have them get out recent pictures and let them create stories from their memories of the pictures. Did you go on vacation? Pull out those pictures, make copies, and pass them out with an instruction to tell you about this picture. Turn those hours of boredom into hours of reliving the happy moments of vacation or school or family time. The activity is personal and interesting to them, and they can be creative as they draw and write. Encourage them to answer questions about the picture and allow their brains the development of memory, perspective, word choices, thoughts, and feelings. You will be happy that they can articulate themselves so well and narrate an event.

After reliving and recording the happy memories, it's time to preserve them. Take it another step further by getting a box and file folders that can hold all the stories. Put the name of each child on a file folder and drop in their folder each picture story they created. This way, you are helping them create their *own* personal history. How fun for them to look back at their pictures and handwriting and memories when they were five, six, seven, eight, nine, and ten years old.

Assign teenagers the same tasks. Instead of you scrapbooking their lives, pull out a few pictures for each year and ask them (or perhaps bribe them) to perform the same action. Teenagers especially need to feel connected and grounded to family. It helps them be safer and think about more than just an immediate moment. It really can strengthen them to withstand peer pressure and prepare them to think with values and higher character traits. The interaction between children and adults helps children mature and make wiser choices.

This is also the time that you can mentor and life coach your children. It gives you the opportunity to express excitement at their successes, joy in the accomplishments, gratitude for the time and money to take vacations, gratitude to the parent that worked hard to provide the finances, and so on. It gives you quality family time to talk.

Elderly adults and children often feel that so much is out of their control. Doing picture and story time with them will give you the moment to sympathize with their situation, build their self-esteem and self-respect, and reframe their perspectives.

It really can be that simple: Fill a boring day with the good memories of our lives. Pictures and stories, together, help us do just that.

ACTION ITEM: Sit down with a family member—whether an older adult, a teenager, or a child—and review pictures together. Write down the basics about the picture, such as the people, the date, and the place. Then, write down the memories and stories behind it.

15

COLLECTING SUCCESS STORIES

*L*et's collect our family's success stories. We can title them "Pivotal Moments," "Life's Lessons," or "Before and After Stories." Whatever we call them, these stories are ones that retell a moment in time that changed someone's life. Even though the experience may only belong to the one person that lived it, all may be able to liken it in their lives as well. Learning from each other, we become unified and empathic to each other. We should be a collector of our family's stories in our hearts, and then we should preserve the collection physically on paper, as well as digitally, to expand its influence.

I think there must be a collector's instinct in all living things. Cows collect around each other in storms. Birds collect shiny objects or pieces of stuff for their nests. Squirrels collect nuts, which is why we use the expression to "squirrel away" something. We talk about collecting money to "save for a rainy day."

As a community we collect books together and call it a library. We collect junk for our junk yards. We collect our money in banks and sometimes in our mattresses. We often collect items for fun or beauty, things like stamps, coins, baseball cards, spoons, postcards, butterflies, bugs, or Christmas Santas. Even people who might insist they collect nothing may have a collection of suits, shirts, ties, socks, or shoes. They may collect businesses, investments, stocks, or bonds. They may collect makeup, perfume, earrings, rings, or necklaces. Even our smallest children collect toy matchbox cars, dinosaurs, dolls, or stuffed animals.

I think we also collect things from our family without even knowing it. Things like attitudes, skills, talents, habits, expressions, mannerisms, and probably a lot more.

I want you to collect stories and family information. A collection can be a collection of lists of data. My grandmother made a list of what everyone died of. She also made lists of family eye color. It would be fun to have a few lists of every living relative's favorite food. If someone kept it going after we were gone, how fun it would be to see favorite foods for 100 years. Some I bet wouldn't even be around anymore. What's a Chi-Chi's taco or a Mighty Casey's hot dog? Do you know what is in Ambrosia Salad or Cream Chipped Beef? My grandfather told me that one of his most often consumed meals as a small child in Alabama (1915–1920) was dry cornbread broken up with buttermilk poured over it for an evening treat. Sounds like the beginning of boxed cereal to me.

People that collect do it all kinds of ways. Some collections feel more like hoarding. Some have a perfectly organized collection. Some have beautiful libraries with bookshelves, and others have books that are stacked all over yet each has a place and can be found.

Some of our collections are truly emotional responses to our childhood. Do you have any of those? Share a picture of your collection and explain on paper why it means something to you. Explain where you acquired some of the items. Share the cost of each item, and most importantly, share the why. *Why* did you collect? This historical reference gives relative insight to you and maybe to other family members as well. I have a sister that stated she did not collect anything. Her children laughed and took a picture of her Christmas decorations that included dozens of the most beautiful nutcracker dolls that she displays each year. My grandmother collected them and passed them on to her, and she has added to it over time.

Some collect family history, and everyone should collect our stories.

I know a wonderful woman, long since gone, that collected stories of our founding fathers. She determined that when she died, if it was possible, she would like to meet George Washington. She had heard so many stories about him and had his portrait in her childhood school rooms. It was a nice thought really. She had a hero, or at least a role model, that had journeyed with her in story form for her ninety years of life. It was only natural that if there was life after death, she had someone special she wanted to meet.

My grandmother collected calendar events. She wrote in each square of her calendar a family moment. We use that collection of calendars to find events in time that would have been lost otherwise. It is her collection of calendars that let us know that on this day in history something important happened in our family.

Let's write success stories of our family in the pivotal moments of their lives. Let's see if we know any life's lessons that our ancestors, relatives, or descendants have. We all should be able to find before and after stories in our lives and in our family's lives.

Find them in living people today before you even try to start going back to the lives of your ancestors. Here again, start with the easiest and first thing that comes to your mind. When was your last success? When was the last success for each of the living family members you have? If you can't think of one, send a text to the person and say, "Hey sibling! What was your last success?" You might just have a wonderful exchange of conversation and learn something about a sibling and be supportive of their successes.

Can you see a success in a perceived failure? Some examples might be: Because of the car accident, I bought a new car. Because I was let go, I found a better job. Because I was left out, I am more aware of others.

Create and gather all the family stories you can so that they may be used by our present and future family for life's lessons, strength, encouragement, comfort, joy, and gratitude.

I have talked to many people over the years that had horrible parenting as they grew up. Even though I extend compassion and understanding to them, I ask them to try to view the past differently. Their parents brought them to life. Their parents taught by negative or poor example, and they now have the opportunity to use that as wisdom to grow and become how a person should be. How else can we change our point of view so that we may benefit, learn lessons, and move toward better?

Maybe it isn't bad parenting but a bad circumstance. Remember the example of Anne Frank, Victor Frankl, Helen Keller, and others. These are people that kept their minds and hearts engaged and broadened their ability to travel though life in a brighter way.

Gathering stories broadens our ability to see and perceive. When we gather lots of stories and frame them by what we learned, how we grew, and how we changed, we have a family story that can strengthen and encourage others. Remember the highest goal of collecting family stories and sharing them is that the stories can be a benefit to all. Our goal is to build more enduring bonds between us. It is to light our way and to light our descendants' way in successfully navigating life.

ACTION ITEM: Begin your own collection of family success stories. Start by writing down your own success stories and pivotal moments. Then, begin reaching out to other family members and record their success stories. Find a way to share these stories with the family.

16

THE FINISHED STORY

*Y*ears ago, my mother and I were driving in the hills of northeast Georgia. We were unsure of our direction when the road changed to a narrow winding one. Each side of the road had either a drop off, a running creek, or a hill. There was no room to turn around and go back. We drove for quite a while and then made a curve that literally skirted around an old home. The porch was so close to the road, we could roll down the windows and touch it.

We were startled that an old gentleman sat in a rocking chair on that porch. Lucky for us, we stopped and asked him which way back to Atlanta. He thought about it for a minute with a kind and helpful face and then said slowly but with great confidence, "You can't get there from here."

Now my mother is a southern country girl herself. Keeping a straight face, she asked, "Where *can* we go that we could get there?"

The man gave some directions and after a little more polite conversation about the day, the weather, and who we were, we drove on. I guess we made it home eventually or we would still be driving around in the wilderness of northern Georgia. That would have been the end of the story.

Now it is a good family story. We still use his phrase, "You can't get there from here." Anytime I am in a jam or face hard decisions, I will tell my mother, "I can't there from here." The wisdom of the story is brought forward. Maybe I really can't get there from where I am, but where can I go so that a solution will present itself? You can't go from first grade to freshmen year college, but you can get there through the process of progressive learning year after year.

You can change the question and then suddenly you have clear directions that you can follow successfully. My mother taught me that perspective—once she reframed the question to the man's perspective, it was then that his answer became helpful. Where could we go so that *then* we could get to Atlanta? There was an answer to *that* question.

Writing family stories may be like that. It's easy to become discouraged when you feel you've got too far to go. Maybe you feel you can't get there from where you are and where your genealogy is. Do not be discouraged. Go to where you *can* go. Do what you can do.

Finding and sharing our family stories is a never-ending journey without a destination and no finish in sight, and that is alright. Enjoy the journey. We will become better people along the way. We will have gathered all within our reach. Someday it will be a hundred years from now and your gathered stories will remain. Maybe like Aesop, it will be a thousand years from now and your stories will be there living in the lives of your posterity and family. They have the possibility to be read by others for hope, encouragement, sorrow, and laughter. They will help your posterity and family have a legacy and an understanding of who you are as a family. They will have the smallest of details (she liked the color red and peppermint ice cream) or the bigger picture (her thoughts and feelings on God).

We are more than we think we are. We have more power for good in our family if we will gather and share our stories and share them in a lasting way on paper. The things we share will become treasured cards, remembrances, pictures, and stories that tie us to all our family. Learn how to create enduring bonds between all our family members that will hold us together and strengthen us for more successes.

Your family story—and your personal story—has the ability to lift, enlighten, and strengthen all your family members if you will become a storyteller. I hope some of your stories will not only make a difference today but will keep doing so for hundreds of years.

～

If you've enjoyed this book, don't forget to read the first in the series, *Share Your Family's Story*. This book is all about adding fun to sharing family history using enriching activities, games, and beautifying projects.

ABOUT THE AUTHOR

Traci Gormley is a family historian and author. With over forty years of experience and dedication to knowing her ancestors, and helping those around her to discover their own, this work is also her passion.

Traci graduated from Brigham Young University with a Bachelor of Arts degree in Family and Community History Studies. She also completed paralegal studies, honing her skills as a researcher.

She has privately published five volumes of her family's history, and she has long loved sharing her knowledge to mentor the people around her.

If you want to keep up with Traci, follow her on Facebook.